To be a Christian is, literally, to be *of Chris* Christian knows, our lives are not automat particularly in a culture, like ours, obsessed with self, dismissive of virtue, and liable to forget God entirely. Derek Vreeland's *Centering Jesus* is a timely and cogent call to refocus our eyes on Christ as the Lamb of God who calls us to witness to his peaceable Kingdom in faith, hope, and love. "Life is hard and humanity continues to invent new ways to compound the difficulties," Vreeland writes, "but I remain hopeful." In *Centering Jesus*, he ably invites readers to share in that hope.

> **BONNIE KRISTIAN**, columnist at *Christianity Today* and author of *Untrustworthy* and *A Flexible Faith*

Living an authentic Christian life within the milieu of consumerism, militarism, and individualism so characteristic of Western culture is among the greatest spiritual challenges of modernity. It's not entirely unlike the challenge faced by the first Christians living in the context of the Roman Empire. Though the challenge is real, the Christian life should always be understood as the thrilling alternative to the world that it is. And this is what makes Derek Vreeland's new book so exciting and timely. *Centering Jesus* provides a series of trail markers for Christian pilgrims who seek to follow the Lamb in the way of life. This book will be an enormous help to all who are yearning for genuine spiritual transformation.

> **BRIAN ZAHND**, author of *When Everything's on Fire*

I've seen Jesus paraded through political arenas like a warhorse. I've watched his name sparkle and fade on screens when celebrities take center stage and peddle his principles. But I've rarely seen Jesus like this—centered, unadorned, except with the glory that is due to the Lamb who sits on the throne. Vreeland cuts through the clutter and helps us catch a glimpse of the Jesus for whom we truly long—the Jesus who can center our lives in grace and peace.

> **TOMMY BROWN**, author of *The Seven Money Types* and *The Ache for Meaning*

Derek Vreeland has named an important truth: Jesus has not been centered in the church's witness. Consequently, the credibility of the church has been severely compromised. But Vreeland doesn't just name this reality. He offers a way forward to help us recapture the beauty of life in Christ. The three-layered framework of spiritual formation, ethics, and our shared life together is a clear and compelling vision to help us recapture our call to center Jesus in all things. I highly recommend this book.

RICH VILLODAS, lead pastor of New Life Fellowship and author of *Good and Beautiful and Kind*

Who would worship a *lamb*? Understandably, we prefer stronger symbols to represent and shape our destinies: strength, power, and victory, not weakness, vulnerability, and sacrifice. Yet in *Centering Jesus*, Derek Vreeland reminds us that the Christian faith envisions a lamb at the center of the throne. Will we follow a God who comes to us not as a fighter but as a lamb? Vreeland writes winsomely, drawing from Scripture, theology, and church tradition to show us how we can behold and bow before the Lamb of God.

CATHERINE McNIEL, author of *Fearing Bravely*

When society finally bottoms out on self-defeating polarization and escalating violence, perhaps it will stop dismissing the reign of a lamb enthroned on a cross as naive and impracticable. Derek Vreeland believes some hearts have had enough and been plowed so deeply as to receive at last the one who sows peace for a harvest of justice. Counterintuitive, yes—but we've tried every alternative to death (literally). Where donkeys, elephants, and eagles inevitably fail, Derek offers us the Lamb who is the Light and Life of the world.

BRADLEY JERSAK, author of the More Christlike trilogy and dean of Theology & Culture at St. Stephen's University

The world is noisy and chaotic. It provokes competition instead of collaboration and hoarding rather than sharing. We constantly need help so that we can love God and others well. Derek Vreeland offers some assistance for living and loving as he weaves together theological ideas, biblical and historical lessons, and personal experiences, all with an astute awareness of contemporary culture, to put a spotlight on Jesus, the Lamb of God. Vreeland's wise, accessible, and thoughtful work gives readers practical guidance for living with Jesus as the center of all of life. *Centering Jesus* decreases the world's background noise and points out ways that we can establish some order from chaos.

DENNIS R. EDWARDS, dean of North Park Theological Seminary

In this politically charged moment marked by hostility, outrage, and division, the church often presents little more than an echo chamber of society. Derek helps the body of Christ retrieve a deeper and more centered allegiance—not in the shape of donkeys or elephants, but with a lamb at the center. He is a guide who has discovered life from the past and is passing it on to better our futures.

AJ SHERRILL, Anglican priest and author of *Being with God*

CENTERING JESUS

How the Lamb of God Transforms
Our Communities, Ethics & Spiritual Lives

DEREK VREELAND

A NavPress resource published in alliance
with Tyndale House Publishers

NavPress is the publishing ministry of The Navigators, an international Christian organization and leader in personal spiritual development. NavPress is committed to helping people grow spiritually and enjoy lives of meaning and hope through personal and group resources that are biblically rooted, culturally relevant, and highly practical.

For more information, visit NavPress.com.

For Leo

May you grow to love and follow the Lamb

CONTENTS

Foreword *xi*

Prelude *xiii*

1. The Curious Case of the Diminishing Lamb *1*
2. Behold the Lamb *17*

   INTERLUDE: SPIRITUAL FORMATION *33*

3. The Jesus Prayer *35*
4. A Jesus-Centered Reading of Scripture *51*
5. The Spirit Points Us to Jesus *67*

   INTERLUDE: CHRISTIAN VIRTUES *81*

6. The Four Sides of Faith *85*
7. Hope in the Age to Come *99*
8. Love in the Way of the Lamb *113*

   INTERLUDE: OUR COMMON LIFE TOGETHER *127*

9. A Jesus Kind of Church *131*
10. Justice in the Peaceable Kingdom of God *147*
11. Not a Donkey or an Elephant but a Lamb *163*

12. The Reign of the Lamb *177*

   Acknowledgments *191*

   Notes *194*

FOREWORD

EARLY IN OUR MARRIAGE, my husband and I lived in a house serving as caretakers for the owners. The home was enormous and beautiful, with soaring glass windows that overlooked a private lake. We often joked that it was the nicest home we would ever live in (it was!), and its crowning jewel, displayed proudly in the center of the first floor, was an antique Steinway grand piano.

The piano was a classic black with real ivory keys. Whenever I slid onto the bench, I half expected Frank Sinatra to materialize beside me and croon. The piano was like a time capsule and a work of art all bound up in one, save for one notable exception: *the sound*. Although this piano was capable of producing transcendent notes, it had not been tuned in years. In its neglected state, the sound came out tinny, dissonant, and harsh.

This is the problem with musical instruments. No matter the quality of their materials, no matter the genius of the masters who crafted them, no matter how conscientiously they are stored, instruments drift. Without regular attention and care, their sound wanders, which is why they require constant retuning.

I occasionally think back on that piano because the human soul is so much the same. The early theologian Saint Augustine understood that every one of us is born *incurvatus in se*—"curved in on ourselves"—until Jesus intervenes in our lives and unbends us, pointing our souls back toward our created end in him. Unfortunately, this is not a one-time fix. If we are left to ourselves, our souls will inevitably drift back to this inward-facing position. That is why we—like a fine musical instrument—must constantly be retuned to, and by, Christ.

However, it's not just our souls that need retuning. When I survey the state of the church right now—the division in our communities, the corruption in our leadership, the individualism in our theology, and the gleeful indulgence of our outrage—there is a jarring dissonance. It is clear to me that our discipleship needs retuning. Christlikeness is not, after all, the sort of thing one stumbles into. Without intentionality, without consistency, and without eyes fixed squarely on the Lamb of God, our souls, our methods, and our institutions will all naturally . . . *drift*.

That is why this book is so important. The message of *Centering Jesus* is a clarion call to radically and dramatically recenter our lives—and our churches—around Jesus, not because we have abandoned him, but because we have crowded him. We cannot possibly tune our souls to Christ amid a cacophony of competing allegiances.

When we fail to center Jesus, we *will* center something or someone else, and I have lived the anxiety and insecurity of that misplaced focus. But I have also experienced the chain-breaking freedom of centering my gaze on Christ alone, which is why I was so eager to write this foreword. Both Derek and I desperately want the same freedom for you.

Sharon Hodde Miller
pastor and author of The Cost of Control

PRELUDE

I RECENTLY WATCHED *ReMastered: Tricky Dick and the Man in Black*, the 2018 documentary about Richard Nixon's invitation to Johnny Cash to perform at the White House in 1970. Nixon wanted to endear himself to white, middle-class America, and he saw Johnny Cash as a way to do that. Cash had released his popular live album *At Folsom Prison* in 1968, and middle America was watching *The Johnny Cash Show* on television. Cash was experiencing a surge in national popularity. Nixon asked Cash to sing familiar country-western songs, but the ever-unpredictable Johnny Cash chose to sing the socially provocative song "What Is Truth," which expressed sympathy for a younger generation asking questions about war. America had closed the door on the 1960s, but civil unrest lingered into the 1970s. War protesters still filled the streets. The war in Vietnam had split the country in two. Governmental leaders, including the president of the United States, were being questioned. The implementation of civil rights policies, including desegregation, was still experiencing backlash. People were angry. Movements of women seeking equal treatment in the workplace and at home continued to challenge social norms. An unsettled tension filled the air. While Johnny Cash stood in the White House prophetically singing about the "lonely voice of youth,"[1] America was experiencing a time of unrest.

The fracture America experienced around the Vietnam War in the 1960s and 1970s continues to creak and crack today. America is still divided. Political leaders are still being held in suspicion. We are still questioning the proper response to racial injustice. The voices of women experiencing abuse continue to fight to be heard. Life in post-pandemic America feels even more uncertain and divided than it did before. Civil discord about legislative policies and public health continues. Vitriol has become the accepted norm, and a clamoring to express our opinions by subjugating and lampooning the views of the other side is now considered acceptable public discourse. Our culture prizes moral outrage over the common good and slanderous rhetoric over common sense. Many of us feel bewildered and exhausted. The illusive silent majority has become the worn-down, weary majority, and we don't know whom to trust. Civic leaders have shown themselves untrustworthy. Business leaders with their eyes on the financial bottom line cannot be trusted. Christian leaders in both evangelical megachurches and established traditional churches continue to disappoint us, leading to a loss of their credibility. Our educational system produces highly educated people whose moral compass is set and reset by social-media trends. Where are we to turn?

I feel somewhat like the disciples of Jesus when, like the crowd around them, they felt bewildered after Jesus talked about eating his flesh and drinking his blood. Many of the crowd turned their backs on Jesus and walked away. Jesus asked his disciples if they wanted to walk away too. Peter responded, "Lord, to whom can we go? You have the words of eternal life" (John 6:68). My instinct during times of confusion and uncertainty has not been so much to push away from Jesus as to draw near to him. I agree with Peter. Where else are we to go? My earliest memories of religion and talk about God were about Jesus. I have been captivated by Jesus since I was a teenager, and amid our uncertainty and division, I am convinced that centering our attention on Jesus is the anchor our souls need.

My desire to write about Jesus comes from the sense of wonder that I still feel in my bones when I reflect on his life, death, resurrection, and ascension. In my pursuit of him, I have been an avid Bible reader, though my consistency in daily Bible reading has ebbed and flowed. Nevertheless, I have lived my adult Christian life close to the words of Scripture. The Bible is, after all, our sacred and inspired text. The Bible is best read as an overarching story with Jesus as the main character. It's inspired truth telling, and it's the most trusted written source we have to see who Jesus is. We do encounter Jesus through prayer and through our participation in the sacraments, but none of those experiences diminish our encounters with Jesus when we open the sacred text.

A few years ago, my daily Bible reading had me in Revelation, perhaps the trickiest New Testament book to read and interpret. As I have taught this book in small groups and in sermons, I often advise people to keep their eyes on Jesus as they are reading through what feels like a stream of consciousness with its moving and fantastic visions and sounds unfolding throughout the text. The opening lines describe the purpose of the book: "The revelation of Jesus Christ" (Revelation 1:1). The book at the end of the New Testament is doing what all Scripture is intended to do—reveal Jesus to us.

My habit over the last few years has been to read through the two-year Daily Office Lectionary readings in a particular translation and then start reading through a new translation when a new two-year cycle begins. One day in late fall before the start of the season of Advent, I was reading from the New Revised Standard Version (NRSV) in Revelation when I encountered these words: "The Lamb at the center of the throne will be their shepherd" (Revelation 7:17). I paused after reading these words because this seemed like fresh language to me. Other translations (such as the KJV, CEB, and ESV) describe the Lamb as being "in the midst of the throne," but the NRSV describes the Lamb as seated in the *center*.

That image lingered in my imagination.

The center.

The Lamb at the center.

As I continued to dwell on that image, I thought, *That is what we need in these unsettled days—the Lamb at the center.* With all the hostility boiling just under the surface of our world, we need a renewed vision of Jesus as the Lamb of God who can lead us in the peaceable ways of the Kingdom. We need renewed practices of centering Jesus in our hearts and minds. With the deep divide in American culture and the polarization that continues to grow, we need a renewed focus on the Lamb, that we might blaze a path forward into civility and kindness.

That next January, I led an online small group entitled "The Lamb at the Center," where I fleshed out these ideas with a few people over nine or ten weeks. This group met during the early days of the COVID-19 pandemic, while many people were homebound. Conversations in that small group formed the structure of this book.

In the following pages, we will imagine together what it looks like to keep Jesus as the Lamb of God at the center of three key areas of our lives—our spiritual formation, our moral lives, and our common life together. Spiritual formation is the work the Holy Spirit does to form us into the image of Jesus. We participate with the Spirit by walking down certain spiritual pathways; particularly for evangelical Christians, those pathways have been Scripture reading and prayer. Centering Jesus in our reading of Scripture and in our life of prayer has become indispensable to healthy Christian spirituality and growth. Our moral lives form the foundation from which we make ethical decisions. We choose what we do and what we say (both in person and on social media) based on who we are. If we are to be Christlike people, then we need a moral center endowed by the virtues of faith, hope, and love. Our common life together underscores God's design for us to live in community—both Christian community and civic society. We need Jesus at the center of our life of congregational worship if the church is to be an alternative society distinct from the division we see in the world. Additionally, if we are to advocate for justice and participate in the topsy-turvy world of political discourse, we need a perspective grounded and centered on King Jesus. This book offers a process for centering Jesus.

Chapter 1 describes the problems we experience when the Lamb is obscured from our view. Chapter 2 walks us through some of the key biblical descriptions of the Lamb. From there we envision the Lamb at the center of those three key areas of our lives mentioned previously. Chapters 3 through 5 walk us through imagining the Lamb at the center of our life of spiritual formation, whereby we discover the Lamb at the center of our prayer life, our devotion to Scripture, and our lived spirituality. Chapters 6 through 8 describe a Lamb-shaped and Jesus-centered approach to the Christian virtues of faith, hope, and love, the foundation of our moral lives. Chapters 9 through 11 lead us through an exploration of the Lamb at the center of our common life together, specifically our worship life, our participation in acts of justice, and our political life. Chapter 12 returns to where we started by envisioning the reigning Lamb in John's revelation.

Each chapter opens with a prayer from *The Book of Common Prayer*. Most of these prayers are collects (pronounced "call-ects"). These are traditional prayers prayed on Sunday mornings during worship gatherings. They are prayers I have grown to appreciate and incorporate in my daily prayers. Before you begin reading a new chapter, I invite you to pray the corresponding prayer out loud. As you read, I pray that you rediscover this ancient and central image of Jesus as the Lamb of God and that in following the Lamb together, we might embody the ways of the Lamb. I believe Jesus is still the hope of the world. He is the reigning Lamb of God who has conquered sin, evil, and death itself. In the words of the Moravian hymn:

Our Lamb has conquered: let us follow him.[2]

The church in North America continues to face criticism and a loss of credibility at a time of deep division and cultural instability. One way to rebuild the church's reputation is by devoting ourselves to centering Jesus in all we do. This book is dedicated to that aim. May the God of peace grant you peace as you read.

Derek Vreeland
GOOD FRIDAY 2022

THE CURIOUS CASE
OF THE DIMINISHING LAMB

Almighty God, you alone can bring into order the unruly
wills and affections of sinners: Grant your people grace to
love what you command and desire what you promise; that,
among the swift and varied changes of the world, our hearts
may surely there be fixed where true joys are to be found;
through Jesus Christ our Lord, who lives and reigns with you
and the Holy Spirit, one God, now and for ever. Amen.

A COLLECT, FIFTH SUNDAY IN LENT,
THE BOOK OF COMMON PRAYER

I'LL BE HONEST. I have very little firsthand experience with
lambs, sheep, or any livestock, for that matter. I grew up in a suburban
neighborhood in the 1980s and early 1990s with pickup games of
basketball, cable TV, and mixtapes. The only farm animals I remember seeing were on TV. The closest I ever came to farm life was in
high school when I would go with my then girlfriend, now wife, to
her grandparents' farm on a breezy hill in northwest Missouri. Visits
to the farm brought up childhood nostalgia for my wife. She has such
fond memories of her grandparents. Her grandfather had been a hog
farmer, but he had long been retired by the time I made my first visit
to the farm. The hogs were long gone, but the pungent smell they left
behind still filled the midwestern air when we visited. On our way
there, we would often pass cows and horses but never sheep or goats.

It wasn't until I grew up and became a pastor that I had the opportunity to experience livestock up close. Every year at our Christmas Eve candlelight service, our church has a live nativity with animals. We have camels, sheep, and if we are lucky, a newborn lamb. One year the family who brings the animals from Oklahoma to our church in Missouri brought a little lamb with them. During the service, costume-clad shepherds led real sheep onto the platform, and a young teenage shepherd carried the lamb in her arms. She sat near the stable on our small set with the lamb on her lap, cuddled in her arms.

Backstage before the service began, the lively lamb innocently and inquisitively explored. On the platform during the service, the lamb, still ever lively, tried to wiggle free from the arms of its teenage shepherd very much like a toddler who was ready to get down and play. As I watched from the front row, I imagined what would happen if that little lamb started running up and down the platform. My heart started to race as I feared the distraction this little lamb could create in the middle of our sacred Christmas Eve service.

My oldest son, all six feet four inches of him, served as one of the shepherds that year and was on the platform when all this was happening. Seeing that the lamb was about to wiggle free from the unsuspecting teenage shepherd, he reached down to take control of our rambunctious little lamb, right as the wise men walked up the platform to present their gifts to baby Jesus. He took hold of the lamb, tucking its miniature legs under its body and holding it close to his chest. Had my son not intervened, my worst fear may have come true. It didn't take much effort for my son to keep the lamb still. He just needed to employ the proper leg-tucking technique. Up against my son and held within his grip, the lamb surrendered and was completely powerless. The suddenly docile lamb looked cute and cuddly. Under a restrictive grip, our little lamb was an unassuming character in our live nativity.

The image of a lamb doesn't evoke feelings of confidence or strength. Sports fans will never hear an announcer say, "Ladies and gentlemen, put your hands together to welcome the mighty Fighting Lambs!" Sports teams want mascots who portray a triumphant persona to form a rallying point for their teams. Plenty of teams proudly go with rams as their mascot, conveying a kind of rugged strength and determination, but none have lamb mascots. Schools and universities want an image to excite their fan base and create a competitive edge. We see bulls, mustangs, broncos, razorbacks, gamecocks, and even ducks (I don't understand that one, University of Oregon fans!), but we never see lambs. Little lambs are simply too harmless and cute to be a team mascot. Despite the cultural aversion to lambs as a symbol of strength and honor, Christians have been given that very image as one of the primary descriptions of Jesus, our reigning Savior and King.

Christians have proclaimed Jesus as the Lamb of God from the beginning. Images of the Lamb have appeared in Christian art since at least the sixth century. The Lamb of God (Latin: *Agnus Dei*) served as an ancient Christian symbol proclaiming the reigning King of kings and Lord of lords in the most humble and unassuming way. Artisans have crafted versions of Jesus as a lamb in stonework, paintings, mosaics, and stained glass. One of the oldest Lamb of God mosaics remaining today flies high above the heads of onlookers at the Italian Church of San Vitale in Ravenna, north of Rome along the Adriatic Sea.[1]

This mosaic appears on the vaulted ceiling, centered above the altar. Ancient craftsmen encircled the lamb mosaic with a wreath denoting the victory of the Lamb. Four angels surround the wreath with hands extending as if they are holding up the Lamb of God. While a victory wreath encircles the Lamb of God in San Vitale, later versions depict the Lamb of God holding a banner bearing a cross. The Moravian Church uses that version of the Lamb of God as their official emblem. Surrounding the banner-bearing lamb is the phrase "Our Lamb has conquered; let us follow him."[2]

The church has included the image of Jesus as the Lamb of God in Christian worship at least since the seventh century, when the liturgical chant "Agnus Dei" was added to Roman Catholic worship. Liturgical churches, such as Anglican, Lutheran, Presbyterian, and others, include prayers and hymns to the Lamb of God. The Great Litany in the Anglican tradition ends with these words:

O Lamb of God, you take away the sin of the world;
>**Have mercy upon us.**

O Lamb of God, you take away the sin of the world;
>**Grant us your peace.**

O Christ, hear us.
>**O Christ, hear us.**

Lord, have mercy upon us.
>**Christ, have mercy upon us.**

Lord, have mercy upon us.[3]

Liturgical congregations are not the only churches incorporating the imagery of the Lamb in their prayers and worship. Evangelical, nondenominational, and Pentecostal/charismatic Christians have been singing "Revelation Song" since Kari Jobe made it popular in 2009. Inspired by images of the Lamb in the book of Revelation, the song opens by praising God using lines from John's vision: "Worthy is the Lamb who was slain."[4] Christians in both traditional and contemporary churches have worshiped Jesus as the Lamb of God, but sadly, a culture that prizes power and pragmatism has dimmed the light on this central image of Jesus. Too many followers of Jesus have lost sight of the Lamb, and in doing so have forgotten the peaceable nature of God's Kingdom.

The church has been inflicted with several diseases. We are divided and unhealthy, unable to be a viable agent of healing to our society. The symptoms are multiple, but I will outline four that I see:

1. The autonomous thinking self pervades the church as a result of people absorbing the enlightenment ideals of America's founders.

2. Militant masculinity has created toxic church cultures led by men who are more shaped by Hollywood violence than the slain Lamb of God.

3. The church's addiction to antagonism has turned the robust body of Christ into a raving and sickly body plagued by infighting.

4. These divisions in the church leave us without a credible witness in the restless culture.

We need to understand these symptoms and why they're happening if we are to have hope for healing. So let's look at each of them here. As we do, we'll better see what kind of cure we need and what the hope of Jesus really looks like.

THE AUTONOMOUS THINKING SELF

The American founders fashioned the American experiment using the framework of the eighteenth-century Enlightenment, where "enlightened" Europeans elevated the individual's ability to reason on their own for the sake of their own interests. This orientation toward the self—toward prioritizing one's own comfort and happiness—occupies a sacred place in American culture, and unfortunately, it has infiltrated the church. Elevation of the individual's ability to think on their own is called the *autonomous thinking self*. This fusion of American-Enlightenment ideals with the values of God's Kingdom is an example of syncretism, a blending of ideas and values from different sources. Syncretism pollutes God's message with falsehoods and causes us to lose our way in our pursuit of God's Kingdom. And it's nothing new.

The silent seduction of syncretism has always been a temptation for the people of God. When we merge the values of the culture around us with the values of God's Kingdom, we look less like God's people and more like the people of a particular culture. The story of Israel reveals our tendency to allow the values of the surrounding culture to seep in and distort our identity as people who worship the one true living God. Resisting the pagan values of nearby people remained a generation-after-generation challenge for the children of Abraham. The God of Israel gave them the law because they were to be a distinct people who belonged to the one true Creator, "a people for his treasured possession" (Deuteronomy 26:18, ESV). God intended the law to form his people into a unique community marked by proper worship and acts of justice—that is, if the Israelites complied.

Yet repeatedly the story of Israel records how often they were influenced by other tribes and nations to worship foreign gods. Their idolatry inevitably led to injustice and immorality as they began to take on the posture and practices of their pagan neighbors. As the Israelites conformed to the image of the peoples around them, they ceased to look like the peculiar people of the God who led them out of slavery in Egypt. Eventually, because of their disobedience, God allowed them to be carried off into exile. Yet that wasn't the end of Israel's story. Many of Abraham's descendants, looking to build a new home in Babylon, kept their distinctiveness as the people of God by remaining Jewish and resisting the cultural pressure to become Babylonian. They worshiped the God of Israel as the creator of all things, and they allowed the law of Moses to shape them. They maintained their unique identity as the holy people of God as they built houses, planted vineyards, got married, and had children in Babylon.

For the church today, as the new-covenant people of God made up of Jews and Gentiles, we are a multiethnic "chosen race, a royal priesthood, a holy nation, a people for his own possession" (1 Peter 2:9, ESV). And we face a similar temptation as ancient Israel. The temptation to absorb the cultural values around us deforms us from people who look like Jesus to people who look like secular, twenty-first-century Americans. We who love God and are called according to God's purposes are being conformed into the image of Jesus (Romans 8:28-29). But without Jesus as the Lamb of God at the center of lives, we become more individualistic, more consumeristic, and more interested in the pursuit of happiness than the principles of biblical justice. Without centering Jesus, we embolden the autonomous thinking self. *We* rule our lives instead of Jesus.

With the autonomous thinking self displacing the Lamb at the center of life and faith, we Christians trust ourselves instead of the Spirit. We lean into the desires of our hearts more than the desires God has for us. We pursue the agendas *we* devise to build the kind of lives that we believe will make us happy. We let the Lamb out to pasture while we stay in the kitchen cooking up what we want. We quickly develop a me-centered approach to Bible reading, where we look to apply select verses to our individual lives. When we do pray, we ask God for what we want. How would people overwhelmed by the influence of individualism and consumerism know anything different? Self-centered people pray self-centered prayers. Our entire spirituality becomes driven *by* the self and *for* the self. We choose which spiritual practices we want to engage in based on how they make us feel. In the end, without the Lamb at the center of our Christian imagination, we find ourselves in a spirituality that uses Christian imagery but works for each isolated individual, one that the modern secular world finds sensible. This kind of pragmatic spirituality replaces faith, hope, and love with me, myself, and I. Centering ourselves on Jesus as the Lamb causes us to bow the knee of our self-understanding to the knowledge of God revealed in the beauty and brightness of King Jesus. With Jesus exalted, we humble ourselves that we may be lifted up (see James 4:10, NLT).

A MILITANT MASCULINITY

A few years ago I led a two-day retreat for some Christian men. We withdrew from our families after work on Friday and took a twenty-four-hour break from our normal day-to-day activities. We met at a Christian retreat center for prayer, conversations, and moments of reflection on living as men echoing the teachings of Jesus. We had great discussions about what it looks like to understand our own sense of masculinity in light of the way of Jesus.

We agreed that we don't want to be a bunch of *dudes*, allowing American cultural images of masculinity to shape our hearts. Neither do we want to take up the convoluted attempts of "biblical masculinity" (because, honestly, there are plenty of men in the Bible we do not want to emulate). We talked about what it would look like to be men like Jesus. *Christian* masculinity was our collective aim. We wanted a masculinity forged in strength, but we wanted to experience a lamb-like strength, the kind of strength marked by self-sacrifice, humility, meekness, and the courage to stand up to bullies in the power of non-retaliation, like Jesus on the cross. I walked away from that retreat realizing that the lack of the Lamb of God in our discipleship makes it far too easy for toxic forms of masculinity to find their way into our churches. Large segments of Christian men—particularly white men within American evangelicalism—have prized what historian Kristin Du Mez calls a "militant masculinity" by idolizing rugged male heroes from television shows and movies. In her book *Jesus and John Wayne: How White Evangelicals Corrupted a Faith and Fractured a Nation*, she explains:

> Although [John] Wayne occupies a prominent place in the pantheon of evangelical heroes, he is but one of many rugged and even ruthless icons of masculinity that evangelicals imbued with religious significance. Like Wayne, the heroes who best embodied militant Christian masculinity were those unencumbered by traditional Christian virtues. In this way, militant masculinity linked religious and secular conservatism, helping to secure an alliance with profound political ramifications. For many evangelicals, these militant heroes would come to define not only Christian manhood but Christianity itself.[5]

As a white Christian man who was raised within American evangelicalism, I understand the draw of militant masculinity. I grew up on action movies from the 1980s, and characters portrayed by Sylvester Stallone and Arnold Schwarzenegger shaped my masculine imagination around images of violence and power. Regrettably I have too easily allowed these action-movie stars to overtake my understanding of Christian manhood, eclipsing the standard of Christian masculinity—Christ Jesus himself!

Men in the church in North America need to have conversations like the one from our two-day retreat because masculinity is being questioned and reimagined these days. The cultural emergence of the abuse and pain caused by toxic masculinity has brought needed scrutiny to not only manhood in general but also Christian manhood. Sexual abuse scandals among leaders in the Catholic church and various evangelical churches have crushed lives and tarnished the beauty of the gospel.

Sadly, in pockets of the church, too many discussions regarding masculinity have echoed the cartoonish and brutish forms of militant masculinity. A few years ago I saw a men's conference video ad featuring fast-moving images of MMA fighters, men shooting automatic weapons, and monster trucks crushing cars. I understand the thinking behind the marketing ploy, and I'm sure they had an arena full of men. I just wondered about the Christian men who weren't attracted to such images of masculinity. Did they attend but feel unseen? Or did they look for a men's conference that better aligned with the kind of masculinity Jesus displayed? I also questioned whether violent imagery allows toxic masculinity to creep into our understanding of what it means to be a Christian man. I'm afraid it does.

The image of Jesus as the Lamb of God reshapes our Christian understanding of masculinity and resists the tough-guy, street-fighter, militant image that so many Christian men have flocked to over the last fifty years. Christian masculinity is forged in strength and struggle, but not the kind of strength that lacks emotional health or empathy.

It's the kind of strength that rejects violence and oppression. Jesus told his disciples: "You know that among the Gentiles those whom they recognize as their rulers lord it over them, and their great ones are tyrants over them. But *it is not so among you*" (Mark 10:42-43, emphasis added). Worldly male leaders then and now know how to use their authority to accomplish tasks. They shut down compassion and vulnerability; put on tough, unflinching faces; and use their authority to push people around. Jesus rejected those kinds of toxic leadership practices. If we collectively forget that Jesus reigns and rules as a slaughtered lamb, we too easily adopt toxic forms of leadership and masculinity. When we work on centering Jesus as the Lamb of God, the stain of militant masculinity is washed clean, freeing men to become more Christlike.

AN ADDICTION TO ANTAGONISM

At the heart of militant masculinity is not a lamb but a lust for power. Without the image of the Lamb, our vision of Jesus easily gets distorted by our attraction to power and control. The idolatry of power corrupts us by causing us to believe the false assumption that the rich and powerful win the game of life. With a power-centric life, Jesus too easily becomes the means by which we secure the power to do what we want. Economic, political, or social power as an idol produces enough moral pollution of its own, but there is a deeper problem.

The haunting truth is that behind the worship of power lies an addiction to antagonism, a multifaceted hostility that seems to rumble and reverberate throughout American culture. According to theologian David Fitch, "Social political life in autonomy from God runs on antagonism."[6] Far from the idealistic dreams of a society held together by "unalienable Rights," "the pursuit of Happiness," and "liberty and justice for all," American democracy is currently driven by the antagonism formed between rich and poor, urban dwellers and country folks, blue states and red states—antagonisms formed by competing views of freedom, justice, and opportunity.[7] Meaningless slogans try to hide the antagonisms, but they remain just below the surface of American life.[8] Political campaigns promote "change," "better days," or "greatness," but these tawdry slogans cover up the truth—in the broken American political system, political gains are secured by cutthroat competition that involves demonizing the other to promote one's own political ideals.

While antagonisms can regrettably spill over into physical violence, they are normally expressed in angry rhetoric, with words chosen as weapons. Both violence and hostile words reveal the sickness of this present age. Jesus radically extended the moral imperative from "You shall not murder" to "if you say, 'You fool,' you will be liable to the hell of fire" (Matthew 5:21-22). Words intended to harm others remain off the table for followers of Jesus just as much as physical weapons used to inflict physical harm. The great influence of Jesus and the church's witness to his life-affirming teachings have suppressed this addiction to antagonism. But domination, exploitation, and acts of rhetorical violence remain with us. We may not literally kill our enemies, but our modern world—particularly our dicey political world—is hooked on the high that comes from slandering our enemies.

Renewing our vision of Jesus as the Lamb rescues us from the addiction to antagonism because as we focus our attention on the peaceable Lamb, we are conformed to that image. We become like that which we behold. We grow into the image we gaze on. We are formed into the person we focus on. We desperately need Jesus as the Lamb at the center of our lives if we are going to preserve the faith and pass it on to the next generation. But we need the real Jesus. We need Immanuel, God with us. We don't need a reinterpreted Jesus, but the one born of the Virgin Mary, the one who suffered under Pontius Pilate. We need the Jesus who was crucified, died, and was buried. We need the Jesus who rose on the third day and ascended to the right hand of the Father.[9] We need Jesus, specifically as the Lamb of God.

Jesus rules and reigns but not in the way of modern rulers. Jesus does not rule by stirring up more antagonism but by flipping the table on hostility. Jesus rules as a lamb not by coercive and manipulative power, but by love. David Fitch adds, "Jesus does not create enemies, but he does disrupt the enemy-making machine and, by doing so, reveals those who love being enemies."[10] Jesus renders useless the enemy-making apparatus and rescues us from the antagonisms that fuel our world. Without the predominance of the Lamb in our churches, antagonisms have room to breathe and can take root in the lives of God's people. With the Lamb at the center, we can truly love one another within the church and practice a kind of love and civility that brings healing and peace to our broken and hostile world.

A DIVIDED CHURCH

Jesus has been building the church into a community of healing where mercy is cultivated for the sake of the world, but when we give antagonisms a foothold in our churches, we become a tribal, enemy-making machine. Sadly this kind of tribalism has taken over congregations in the US. Americans have created divided tribes identified by whom they are against. Jesus came as our peaceable, lamb-like Shepherd, breaking down "the dividing wall, that is, the hostility between us" (Ephesians 2:14), but the church itself has rebuilt that wall and restored the hostility Jesus came to save us from. When we lose sight of the Lamb, we lose our peace, and then local churches entrench themselves in a tribal warfare where they are known more for what they are against than for what they are for.

The Protestant Reformation, which began in the sixteenth century, was inevitable. The church in Western Europe had become corrupt, so Martin Luther nailed his Ninety-Five Theses to the door of the castle church in Wittenberg, Germany, marking a watershed moment in the history of the Protestant church. Luther wanted a theological debate; what he got was a revolution. The movement sparked by Luther in Germany spread throughout Europe, erupting in new protest movements. These new Protestant traditions, including the Anabaptist radical reformers, brought new life to the church, elevating the sacred nature of Scripture and restoring King Jesus to the throne. But what began as one fracture in the Western church turned into thousands of fractures, particularly as the gospel spread through North America in the eighteenth and nineteenth centuries. So while we rejoice in the attempts at reformation, we also lament the ongoing fracturing of the church.

Today churches in the US divide over not only doctrine, like in the Reformation, but also ethnicity, worship styles, politics, methodology, leadership, traditions, and, at times, ego and pride. Fitch describes how warring church tribes wave metaphorical banners. Slogans like "biblical truth" and "biblical values" get waved around, but they are often little more than empty slogans that sound Christian but are vacant of meaning.[11] The truth and values we derive from the Bible must be clearly defined, otherwise our sacred Scriptures get weaponized. Verses are removed from their respective contexts and launched as missiles to destroy tribes who are "obviously" wrong and violating "biblical truth." Holy Scripture is too sacred to be reduced to bullets in our theological guns. Scanning the Bible for a verse or two that helps prove our point of view undermines the purpose of Scripture: to bear witness to Jesus, the living and reigning Word of God. Without the Lamb as our Shepherd, we sheep go to war with one another, fueling the "us versus them" mentality in present-day American culture.

When the Lamb disappears from our eyes, the light of Jesus' prayer for unity in John 17 grows dim. For the disciples then and for us now, Jesus prayed, "that they may all be one. As you, Father, are in me and I am in you, may they also be in us, so that the world may believe that you have sent me" (John 17:21). Jesus wants the church to experience a oneness similar to the unity the Holy Trinity experiences. But our contentious spirit delays Jesus' prayerful vision from becoming actualized on earth. With Jesus back at the center, we have hope for a united church where we love one another with brotherly affection despite our denominational differences.

In the face of radical individualism, militant masculinity, rapidly spreading antagonisms, and a fractured church, we need King Jesus who rules and reigns as the Lamb of God. We desperately need the Lamb of God at the center of our lives. We need an overhauled imagination where we begin to imagine Jesus conquering not by slaying his enemies but by being slain. We need to see Jesus with fresh eyes, envisioning him as "the Lamb who was slaughtered before the world was made" (Revelation 13:8, NLT). When we catch a glimpse of this Lamb of God, we will begin to see all these symptoms—our autonomy, our view of masculinity, our antagonisms, our division—in a new light. When we see the Lamb who was slain, all these things will be put in their rightful place. And we will find ourselves becoming the people God has created us to be. So we turn our eyes now to behold the Lamb.

DISCUSSION QUESTIONS

1. What is your experience with farm animals?

2. What is the first thing that comes to mind when you imagine Jesus as a lamb?

3. What do we lose if we lose sight of Jesus as the Lamb of God?

4. What damage can happen to our faith if we place ourselves instead of Jesus at the center of our lives?

5. How can Jesus serve as the remedy to militant masculinity?

6. Have you personally experienced the hostility and antagonisms in our world? If so, what was that experience like?

7. Have you experienced a church conflict? How was that situation resolved?

8. What is one thing you can do to center your faith on Jesus as the Lamb of God?

BEHOLD THE LAMB

Lord Jesus Christ, only Son of the Father,
Lord God, Lamb of God,
you take away the sin of the world:
have mercy on us;
you are seated at the right hand of the Father:
receive our prayer.

For you alone are the Holy One,
you alone are the Lord,
you alone are the Most High,
Jesus Christ,
with the Holy Spirit,
in the glory of God the Father. Amen.

DAILY MORNING PRAYER: RITE TWO,
THE BOOK OF COMMON PRAYER

I CAN RECALL the weakness in my knees when I saw my wife walking down the aisle on our wedding day. We followed the tradition of not seeing one another that day until the ceremony had begun. We have always been casual-T-shirt-and-jeans kind of people. So when I saw her in her beautiful white dress, hair flowing down in curls, eyes sparkling as they met mine, I was captivated. I stood motionless and watched as she walked toward me.

Occasionally life presents us with moments that feel so awe-inspiring, so breathtaking, that we feel compelled to stop and just look. We rarely experience these kinds of beautiful moments in our day-to-day lives. When we do, we tend to be outdoors. We stand in awe when we catch the sun melting into the horizon at the beach. We gaze at a distant mountain vista that peeks out at us through a densely wooded area. We turn our attention to the bursting of colors as the leaves go from green to vibrant oranges, reds, and yellows in autumn. We treasure these moments as we stop to impress the beauty on our hearts and in our minds.

King David composed a psalm expressing this same sentiment: "One thing I asked of the LORD, that will I seek after: to live in the house of the LORD all the days of my life, to behold the beauty of the LORD, and to inquire in his temple" (Psalm 27:4). To behold the beauty of the one true God of creation is to gaze on the creator of all things beautiful and breathtaking. God, who is love, has woven love into all creation, particularly into humanity, so that we might see love all around us.

Nothing in all creation reveals the love of God more clearly than the Son of God, Jesus, who came into the world to show us what God is like. Jesus came to demonstrate God's love "in that while we still were sinners Christ died for us" (Romans 5:8). When John the Baptist saw Jesus approaching him, he proclaimed, "Behold, the Lamb of God, who takes away the sin of the world!" (John 1:29, ESV). Jesus died to defeat sin and death for us, and he did so as the Lamb of God. And when we see Jesus in all his gloriousness, we do believe. But before we believe in him, first we *behold him*. We trust in all of Jesus' redeeming work for us and for the world. We receive this work of redemption so that through it, the Holy Spirit might create new life within us. But we don't want to use Jesus to be saved; we want to stop and look because a moment of wonder inspires a lifetime of worship.

So who is this Jesus who inspires both wonder and worship? John the Baptist was convinced that Jesus was both the Son of God and the Lamb of God. These two titles show us a Jesus who reigns *and* a Jesus who was slain. And the link between them helps us become aware that Jesus is even more wonderful than we had imagined.

John testified that Jesus is the one who comes baptizing with the Holy Spirit (John 1:33). Jesus had come as the only begotten Son of God, sent by the Father in the power of the Spirit. As the Son of the Father, Jesus came with the promise that God would "make the nations your heritage, and the ends of the earth your possession" (Psalm 2:8). The title "Son of God" in this sense was not to indicate that Jesus was the second person of the Trinity, although that is true. To people in the first-century Greco-Roman world, the phrase "Son of God" referred to an earthly leader.[1] Jesus as the Son of God came as a leader who would rule the nations the Father gave him.

His rule wouldn't be conducted in the way of pagan kings and tyrants, however. Jesus came to rule as a lamb. He rules as the sacrificed Lamb who takes away the sin of the world. His strength as a king is not rooted in self-aggrandizing power but in self-sacrificing love. He does not use his power to coerce and manipulate followers. He *gives* his power away through the Holy Spirit, so we as his followers are empowered to live lives reflecting his beautiful life.

Jesus is the Son of God who reigns by having become the Lamb of God. As the one with all authority in heaven and earth, Jesus leads by the power of self-sacrificing love. In this regard, Jesus is both a shepherd and a lamb. He came to lead and to offer himself as a sacrifice that we may be liberated from sin, evil, and death. He came to rule the nations as the world's true King, and he also came to sacrifice himself for the sin of the world. Jesus reigns in God's Kingdom, enabling men and women to enter it.

So why is it important to behold the Son of God as the Lamb of God? Because it makes us more like him. As human beings, we tend to take on characteristics of whatever or whomever we focus on. We are formed by those people, objects, and ideas that receive our attention. Becoming like Jesus is the goal of our lives as Christians. And if Jesus is the Lamb of God, then we must behold him as such to become like him. As we do, we will find that the problems of the autonomous thinking self, militant masculinity, an addiction to antagonism, and a divided church begin to diminish.

John the Baptist declared Jesus to be the Lamb of God and we, too, can behold him as we keep our eye out for the Lamb throughout the story Scripture tells.

THE LAMB IN THE PASSOVER

Jesus as the Lamb of God was prefigured in the Passover lamb of the Exodus. The first Passover was the divine response to the deep injustice experienced by God's people, the Hebrews. At that time, the people of God found themselves the enslaved labor force of the Egyptian Empire. As the Hebrews multiplied in number, the Egyptians worked them mercilessly. With great disdain masking his fear, the pharaoh went so far as to order the Egyptians to throw all newborn Hebrew boys into the river. But God saw their oppression. God heard their cries. The cruel injustice of it all prompted the God of Israel to action.

To prepare the Hebrews for their exodus from slavery, God gave Moses and Aaron, Israel's leaders, the following instructions involving a lamb:

> Tell all the congregation of Israel that on the tenth day of this month every man shall take a lamb according to their fathers' houses, a lamb for a household. . . . Your lamb shall be without blemish, a male a year old. You may take it from the sheep or from the goats, and you shall keep it until the fourteenth day of this month, when the whole assembly of the congregation of Israel shall kill their lambs at twilight.
> EXODUS 12:3, 5-6, ESV

These guidelines helped the Israelites prepare what would become the Passover meal. The blood of the lamb would play a specific role in their exodus. God continued:

Then they shall take some of the blood and put it on the two
doorposts and the lintel of the houses in which they eat it.
They shall eat the flesh that night, roasted on the fire; with
unleavened bread and bitter herbs they shall eat it.
EXODUS 12:7-8, ESV

The blood of the lamb was applied to the sides and top of the
doorframe of their homes so that when the Destroyer came bringing
death, he would pass over the homes marked by the blood. The death
of the firstborn was God's judgment on Egypt (Exodus 12:12). The
Hebrew people would not fall under the same judgment. The blood
of the lamb would rescue them from the Destroyer.[2] Centuries later
Jesus would come as the Passover Lamb to save us all from the specter
of death. Paul invoked this image of Jesus while exhorting the church
in Corinth to repent of sexual immorality:

Christ, our Passover Lamb, has been sacrificed for us.
So let us celebrate the festival, not with the old bread of
wickedness and evil, but with the new bread of sincerity
and truth.
1 CORINTHIANS 5:7-8, NLT

Jesus, the Passover Lamb, was sacrificed for us, for our sin, so that
we can be cleansed and liberated from the wages of sin, which is death
itself (Romans 6:23). Peter used similar language:

You know that God paid a ransom to save you from the
empty life you inherited from your ancestors. And it was not
paid with mere gold or silver, which lose their value. It was
the precious blood of Christ, the sinless, spotless Lamb
of God.
1 PETER 1:18-19, NLT

This spotless Lamb offers his precious blood so that we may be "cleansed by the blood of Jesus Christ" (1 Peter 1:2, NLT).

John the Baptist, who came to prepare the way for the Lord, declared that Jesus is the Lamb of God. John drew on the imagery of the lamb from the story of Israel. Jesus punctuated John's declaration when he shared his final meal with his disciples before his death:

> As they were eating, Jesus took bread, and after blessing it broke it and gave it to the disciples, and said, "Take, eat; this is my body." And he took a cup, and when he had given thanks he gave it to them, saying, "Drink of it, all of you, for this is my blood of the covenant, which is poured out for many for the forgiveness of sins."
> MATTHEW 26:26-28, ESV

The church's practice of Communion draws on this picture of Jesus as the Passover Lamb. Jesus' very blood would be the blood of the covenant. Sins would be forgiven, signaling the end of exile for God's people and the beginning of a new life. The blood of Jesus would be the blood of the Passover Lamb, provided by God to usher in the beauty of God's new creation.

THE LAMB IN ISAAC'S STORY

Even before the Passover Lamb and the Exodus from Egypt, we find the Lamb standing in as a means of God's mercy for humankind. God's plan to save the world begins with the covenant he made with Abraham. God promised Abraham a great family, one that would eventually become a great nation: "I will make of you a great nation, and I will bless you, and make your name great, so that you will be a blessing. . . . In you all the families of the earth shall be blessed" (Genesis 12:2-3). Through that great nation God would bless all the nations of the earth, a blessing ultimately fulfilled in Jesus. God's covenant with Abraham carried with it the very salvation of the world.

God blessed Abraham and Sarah with a child in their old age. They laughed out loud when they learned that they were going to have a baby (Genesis 17:17; 18:12). Following God's direction, they named their son Isaac, which means "laughter." They loved Isaac. And the promised great nation would come through him.

Then God told Abraham to sacrifice Isaac, this son of promise. We can only imagine the shock Abraham felt when God told him to take Isaac to Mount Moriah and sacrifice him there (Genesis 22:2). How could Abraham believe that the God who gave him a son was now telling him to offer that son as a sacrifice? How could Abraham go through with it? How could Abraham's family become a great nation without Isaac?

This human sacrifice would be a burnt offering, a perplexing act of worship for Abraham. Animals were sacrificed to the Lord, not children! Nonetheless, he loaded Isaac, some wood, and two servants and went to the mountain. After traveling for three days, they arrived. Abraham left the servants with his donkey, stoically placed the wood on Isaac, and proceeded a bit further up the mountain. While they made their way to the place of sacrifice, Isaac broke the silence to ask: "Behold, the fire and the wood, but where is the lamb for a burnt offering?" (Genesis 22:7, ESV). Isaac asked a legitimate question. He knew how sacrifices worked. First, one built an altar out of wood, and then some kind of animal—often a lamb—would be sacrificed on the altar. Abraham responded, "God will provide for himself the lamb for a burnt offering, my son" (Genesis 22:8, ESV). As we will see shortly, God won't allow Isaac to be killed. God will provide a lamb for Abraham to use instead.

Abraham built the altar from the wood Isaac had carried. Once the altar was constructed, he laid his beloved son on it. He pulled out the razor-sharp knife he had packed and slowly raised it over his head. Isaac's eyes grew large in surprise. Abraham held his breath. Then suddenly the angel of the Lord spoke from heaven, "Do not lay your hand on the boy or do anything to him, for now I know that you fear God, seeing you have not withheld your son, your only son, from me" (Genesis 22:12, ESV). Abraham lifted his eyes. He heard something rustling nearby. His eyes fell on a ram caught in a thicket by his horns. Abraham continued with the sacrifice, but he offered the ram instead of his son. God had indeed provided the lamb, just as Abraham had said he would. This emotional scene revealed to Abraham—and reveals to us—that God doesn't want human sacrifice.

When we look for Jesus in the story of Isaac, we find him in the ram caught in the thicket. Jesus is the sacrificial Lamb of God, provided by God the Father, who takes sin away so that God's image-bearing creatures can live as new people. We are washed clean by the blood of Jesus and made fully alive in him.

We see Jesus as the Lamb of God forecasted in Isaac's story and in the Passover event of Exodus. We also hear Jesus proclaimed as the Lamb of God in John's Gospel, but nowhere do we see Jesus more radiantly displayed as the Lamb of God than in the last book in all Holy Scripture, Revelation. Let's look for the Lamb there.

THE LAMB IN JOHN'S REVELATION

The revelation given to John as recorded in the book of Revelation is first and foremost the revelation of Jesus Christ. It's not the revelation of the Antichrist, the end times, or that vaccines are the mark of the Beast. What we have been given is a revelation of Jesus Christ as the grand finale of the big story Scripture is telling. In fact, Revelation 1 opens with these words: "The revelation of Jesus Christ." God offers this revelation "to show to his servants the things that must soon take place" (Revelation 1:1, ESV).

God desired for the first-century church to know (through cryptically symbolic language) that the mighty Roman Empire was a beast full of false prophets and consumed by evil and abominations. But the good news was that God would free his people from this tyranny. Judgment was coming to the Roman Empire, much like it had come to ancient Babylon.

Regrettably the book of Revelation has been misused in terrible ways. Throughout history, church leaders have borrowed certain imagery from the book to vilify their enemies. For hundreds of years Protestant groups have tried to predict the end of the world using the book of Revelation. They always get it wrong, *obviously*. Today some evangelicals try to match current events with passages in Revelation, attempting to save people from pending destruction. They share their short-sighted interpretations of Revelation so that unsuspecting Christians and sinners aren't swept up in some kind of end-times calamity. This kind of interpretation is not how to best engage with this apocalyptic book.

Reading Revelation is much like interpreting a political cartoon. Imagine one with an elephant and a donkey standing on their hind legs, facing one another with human-like scowls. Imagine they are wearing boxing shorts and boxing gloves, and the caption reads: "The fight continues." As a modern American, you easily understand the symbols. You don't see the cartoon and think that elephants and donkeys are literally going to start boxing. Rather you know it depicts the current state of the country's politics.

Revelation is filled with important symbols and moving imagery that require interpretation. It's a unique style of writing, much different than the Gospels or Paul's letters. Interpreting many of the symbols in Revelation requires a working knowledge of first-century Roman and Jewish cultures. In reading Revelation, we don't take the imagery found in these layered visions literally. The chapters are filled with symbols that point to a deeper meaning. Let's look at that deeper meaning by focusing our attention on a primary symbol from the book: the Lamb.

THE LION IS A LAMB

John the Revelator sees a scroll with seven seals. The opening of these seals has taken center stage in some interpretations of the book of Revelation, but locating Jesus in Revelation requires focusing not on the scroll itself but on the one who is able to open it. Drama breaks out in John's vision when no one in heaven or earth is worthy to break the seals and open the scroll. This obstacle moves John to tears. He writes:

> I began to weep loudly because no one was found worthy
> to open the scroll or to look into it. And one of the elders
> said to me, "Weep no more; behold, the Lion of the tribe of
> Judah, the Root of David, has conquered, so that he can
> open the scroll and its seven seals."
> REVELATION 5:4-5, ESV

Good news! The Lion of the tribe of Judah is worthy. He can open the scroll.

John turns to look, but he doesn't see a lion. He sees something different: "Between the throne and the four living creatures and among the elders I saw a Lamb standing, as though it had been slain, with seven horns and with seven eyes, which are the seven spirits of God sent out into all the earth" (Revelation 5:6, ESV). Instead of a lion, John saw a lamb.

Jewish people living in the first century longed for the return of the King, the appearance of the Jewish Messiah who would rule in preeminence like King David. The Lamb in John's vision who was worthy enough to open the scroll is revealed as Israel's lion, a king in the lineage of David. The surprise in this vision is that this roaring king is in fact a lamb—one that looks like it has been slain. This is the Lamb of God, who takes away the sin of the world. When the kingly Lamb takes the scroll, the four creatures and the twenty-four elders fall down in worship (Revelation 5:8).

Despite its appearance, the Lamb doesn't lack power, but this vision of a lamb challenges the conventional understanding of power known in the first century and today. According to New Testament scholar Michael Gorman, "In Revelation the nature of power is being redefined. The power of the Lamb in Revelation takes two forms: the power of his death, the symbol of which is the slaughtered lamb, and the power of his spoken word, the symbol of which is the sword of his mouth."[3] The Lamb's power is not in the ability to devour his enemies (though he has that) but in his sacrificial love, the kind that suffers with us. The Lamb's words slay the wicked with the truth of the gospel. The Lamb of God rules by love and truth rather than by coercion and force.

WORSHIP OF THE LAMB

One of the central orientations to the Lamb in John's revelation is that of devotion and worship. We follow Jesus as the Lamb of God, and the Lamb is also worthy of our worship. In fact, our worship of Jesus provides energy for our pursuit of him. When the disciples encountered the resurrected Jesus before receiving the great commission, their first response was worship (Matthew 28:17). Such worship energizes our mission today.

The Lamb is worshiped throughout the book of Revelation, giving us a pattern to follow. In response to one such heavenly vision, John writes:

> Then I looked, and I heard around the throne and the
> living creatures and the elders the voice of many angels,

numbering myriads of myriads and thousands of thousands, saying with a loud voice,

> "Worthy is the Lamb who was slain,
> to receive power and wealth and wisdom and might
> and honor and glory and blessing!"

And I heard every creature in heaven and on earth and under the earth and in the sea, and all that is in them, saying,

> "To him who sits on the throne and to the Lamb
> be blessing and honor and glory and might forever
> and ever!"

REVELATION 5:11-13, ESV

The religious and political powers attempted to humiliate and discredit Jesus by crucifying him, but Jesus' death became a moment of redemption. According to New Testament professor Dana Harris, "Because of this redemptive act, the hymn of praise to God the creator changes to a hymn of praise for God the Redeemer."[4] This heavenly picture of worship spills over to the earth and even under the earth and in the sea. The Lamb who was slain is worthy of all praise from all creation.

The angels and the heavenly elders all worship the Lamb as God and King. Attributes like power, honor, and glory were given to kings in the ancient world. Now they are given to the Lamb. This scene is a small picture of the gospel. In and through Jesus, the God of creation has become the reigning King of heaven and earth.

These images of the Lamb in Revelation likely draw from Daniel's vision. Daniel saw one who came like a Son of Man, a title that Jesus would later use to describe himself. Concerning this Son of Man, Daniel says, "to him was given dominion and glory and a kingdom,

that all peoples, nations, and languages should serve him; his dominion is an everlasting dominion, which shall not pass away, and his
kingdom one that shall not be destroyed" (Daniel 7:14, ESV). The
Son of Man from Daniel's vision is similar to Isaiah's prophecy of the
coming Jewish King, the Messiah, who would be called Wonderful
Counselor, Mighty God, Everlasting Father, and the Prince of Peace
(see Isaiah 9:6). "Of the increase of his government and of peace
there will be no end," Isaiah writes, "on the throne of David and over
his kingdom, to establish it and to uphold it with justice and with
righteousness from this time forth and forevermore" (Isaiah 9:7, ESV).
The Lamb who is worshiped in Revelation is the Son of Man and the
Prince of Peace. The Lamb in John's vision pulls together both images.

For first-century Jewish people, these prophetic images reinforced
the idea that the Lamb is clothed in power and worthy of worship.
The Lamb in John's revelation is again worshiped as he breaks open
the first six seals of the scroll:

> After this I looked, and behold, a great multitude that no one
> could number, from every nation, from all tribes and peoples
> and languages, standing before the throne and before the
> Lamb, clothed in white robes, with palm branches in their
> hands, and crying out with a loud voice, "Salvation belongs
> to our God who sits on the throne, and to the Lamb!"
> REVELATION 7:9-10, ESV

The "great multitude" represents the multiethnic people of God
who have entered God's Kingdom according to his eternal purpose.
God desired from the beginning to have a big multiethnic family. As
the embodiment of Israel, Jesus fulfills this ancient desire and dream,
and as the Lamb of God, Jesus has redeemed and blessed a unified
family who worships the one true living God.

From the ram in the thicket to the first Passover to the promise of the Lamb's reign, we behold King Jesus in this counterintuitive form: a slaughtered lamb. Don't just glance at him—gaze at him. We have to slow down to properly behold the Lamb and allow that image to be imprinted on our souls. Pastor and author John Mark Comer writes, "If we can slow down both—the pace at which we think and the pace at which we move our bodies through the world—maybe we can slow down our *souls* to a pace at which [we] can 'taste and see that the LORD is good.'"[5] Once we slow down we can see that Jesus, the peaceable and humble Lamb of God, is good, and he is leading us toward the good life.

Centering Jesus as the slain Lamb of God allows us to displace the autonomous thinking self with the Lamb on the throne. John's revelation wipes our imagination clear of our obsession with ourselves. The image of a lamb is the antidote to militant masculinity. Men who want to pursue Christian masculinity cannot look past this image of Jesus as the Lamb who conquers not with violent strength but by being slain. Jesus' willingness to suffer and die is the opposite of masculine weakness. The Cross of Jesus reveals the strength of restraint, the strength of suffering, and the strength of sacrifice for the benefit of others. Centering Jesus in our minds as the Lamb of God who takes away the sin of the world causes the toxic air of antagonism to dissipate, leaving us with nothing but peace and charity for those we consider our enemies. Finally, the only hope we have for a unified church, healed of our centuries-old divisions, is for us all to look to the Lamb of God. The humility of the Lamb leads us to humble ourselves before one another. The blood of the Lamb washes us clean of past guilt and hurt so we can love one another as brothers and sisters in the body of Christ.

As followers of Jesus, we want to keep the Lamb at the center of all we do, but this is particularly critical in three areas: our lives of spiritual formation, our moral lives, and our lives lived in community. All that we do as moral beings and all that we do in our communities are shaped by our formational habits, especially prayer and Scripture reading. We will consider what it means for us to keep Jesus at the center of our prayer life and how centering Jesus in our Scripture reading helps us make sense of the big story the Bible is telling. We will look at the Holy Spirit's work of forming us into Jesus' image and directing our attention to Jesus. These formational acts set the stage for a review of faith, hope, and love, virtues that form our internal moral compass. We will find Jesus at the heart of these ancient virtues. Then we will examine the necessity of centering Jesus in our worship lives, in our advocacy for justice for all, and in our political engagement. Let's turn our attention now to the art of spiritual formation.

DISCUSSION QUESTIONS

1. What is one of the most beautiful things you have ever seen? What made it so beautiful?

2. What is the value of not only trusting Jesus in his redeeming work but also taking the time to behold him with awe and wonder?

3. As our Passover Lamb, what does Jesus save us from?

4. What is the significance of seeing God as the one who provides the lamb for Abraham to sacrifice instead of Isaac?

5. What value do you find in reading the book of Revelation as the revelation of Jesus and not a revelation of the end of the world?

6. What does the image of the slain Lamb in Revelation communicate to us about how Jesus reigns?

7. What do you notice about worship around the throne in Revelation?

8. What is one thing you can do this week to slow down and ponder the beauty and wonder of Jesus, the Lamb of God?

SPIRITUAL FORMATION

AS WE BEHOLD the Lamb of God, we find ourselves becoming more like him, because as we consistently focus our attention on a certain image, we discover characteristics of that image becoming imprinted on our hearts. Unlike pesky dandelions, which seemingly grow overnight, we don't grow in Christlikeness suddenly. Rather we grow more like mighty oak trees. We become more like Jesus over a lifetime of intentional spiritual formation.

We love to cling to the great promise found in Romans 8:28, "We know that all things work together for good for those who love God." The promise of God's providential hand causing all things to work together for our good has brought hope to Christians throughout the centuries, but often we have cut our reading too short. The rest of the verse reveals that this promise is made to those "who are called according to his purpose." What is that purpose? We find the answer in the next verse. "Those whom he foreknew he also predestined to be conformed to the image of his Son, in order that he might be the firstborn within a large family" (Romans 8:29).

The purpose for which we are called, the purpose wherein we find true, lasting peace, is being conformed into the image of God's own Son, the Lamb of God, who takes away the sin of the world. According to philosopher and writer Dallas Willard, spiritual formation is a "Spirit-driven process of forming the inner world of the human self in such a way that it becomes like the inner being of Christ himself."[1] What makes spiritual transformation "spiritual" is that it is the work of the Holy Spirit. We can choose to work in harmony with the Spirit or against the Spirit, hindering this process. The way we work with the Spirit is through the practice of the classic disciplines, what I have called "spiritual pathways."[2]

I imagine spiritual pathways to be well-worn trails blazed through the dense forest of the Christian faith. It is true that new disciplines can put us in places where we can be formed by the Spirit, but I prefer old paths. I prefer to walk down pathways that have been time-tested and vetted over the centuries. Now, I have my suspicions about the longevity of Christian fads and trends. I am in favor of innovations. There are times to blaze new trails; but first we must master the old ones. Two pathways that Christians have walked on the road following the Lamb are prayer and Scripture reading—and the Holy Spirit meets us through both. As we consider those two spiritual pathways, we want to develop practices of centering Jesus in them. We want to imagine them with Jesus as the Lamb of God at the center.

In the next three chapters, we turn our attention to answer these three questions: How do we shape our prayer life around Jesus? How do we read all Scripture with Jesus at the center? And what is the Spirit doing to lead us to Jesus in all this?

THE JESUS PRAYER

O God, whose glory it is always to have mercy: Be gracious
to all who have gone astray from your ways, and bring them
again with penitent hearts and steadfast faith to embrace
and hold fast the unchangeable truth of your Word, Jesus
Christ your Son; who with you and the Holy Spirit lives and
reigns, one God, for ever and ever. Amen.

A COLLECT, SECOND SUNDAY IN LENT,
THE BOOK OF COMMON PRAYER

CHRISTIANS INSTINCTIVELY KNOW that prayer is a necessary
component to a vibrant relationship with the God who is a relational
community—the Father, Son, and Holy Spirit. Prayer is a sacred space
where the Spirit forms our hearts in the ways of the Lamb of God. Yet
too many followers of Jesus lack consistency in prayer, and they often
feel ashamed of that. They hear a sermon or listen to a podcast on
prayer, and they sprint out of the gate blazing new pathways of prayer
with the best of intentions, but then life happens. Stress, distractions,
or sheer boredom settles in, and times of prayer become sporadic.
Then these Jesus followers are left feeling ashamed again. To ignore
feelings of guilt, they drift into apathy, which produces an anemic
spirituality. Does any of this sound familiar? Sadly I know the feelings
of guilt, apathy, and spiritual anemia. For far too long I experienced

no lasting consistency in my prayer life. It took me years—decades, in fact—before I learned to pray with life-giving regularity.

God has given us prayer as a simple, subtle way to remain connected to God. We do not progress in our pursuit of the Lamb—with an openness to the gentle presence of the Holy Spirit conforming us to the lamblike image of Jesus—without a habit of life-giving prayer. Forming words to communicate with the God of creation and sitting quietly in God's presence are both foundational practices to our life of faith. As you likely know from experience, relationships require the intentionality of being in each other's presence and communicating with each other. Think of the number of failed marriages that have occurred where the couple simply drifted apart because they stopped spending quality time together and all attempts at meaningful communication faded away. We will struggle to have a healthy relationship with anyone if we are not present and if we don't communicate. For that reason, prayer is essential.

Prayer cultivates an awareness of God's presence. This must be a priority for us to withstand the rising floodwaters of secularism, which threaten to sweep us into a future where God is reduced to a mascot or a social construct. Those of us who are following Jesus in North America have been watching the rising tide of secularism expand not only in civic life but also in church life. *Secularism* can be defined as those ways we attempt to live life without God. It's a worldview which has elevated the autonomous thinking self and technology to such a height that the possibility of a living and active God seems like an afterthought. We Christians have already become more secular than we recognize or care to admit. These floodwaters threaten to overtake us and sweep away the foundations of our shared faith in Jesus. God has given prayer to us as an age-old life preserver that can keep us from drowning. Prayer is about carving out time and space to cultivate an awareness of the presence of God, who is ever present in the world he loves, in this place we call home. We need a renewal of this kind of practice.

While people like me continually struggle with developing a consistent, vibrant prayer life, I have encountered people over the years who have an uncanny bent toward spirituality and prayer. These ordinary Christians are true mystics who have hearts and minds drawn to prayer and the presence of God. They approach Christian spirituality with ease because they have the kind of personality that seems to fit the practices of silence, solitude, stillness, prayer, and contemplation. Some of these spiritual savants can be found in monasteries around the world. Others are found in prayer chapels and Sunday school rooms in rural, out-of-the-way little churches. I have great respect for the mystics among us, but I freely admit that I'm not one of them. I'm among the spiritually poor, that is, those who are simply poor at being spiritual. Luckily for me, and for so many others, in the Beatitudes Jesus proclaimed, "Blessed are the poor in spirit, for theirs is the kingdom of heaven" (Matthew 5:3).

In the past I avoided praying daily and devotionally because, to be completely honest, I didn't know how to pray. As a pastor, I could pray for other people in need. I could pray within the context of a worship service. But alone, in my room with the door closed, I didn't have the words to say. Furthermore when I did pray, I experienced disappointment with God when I did not receive what I wanted. More than once I wondered if prayer was a waste of time. Questioning and doubt opened the door for the stress and the busyness of life to overrun the thought of prayer. I used all the typical excuses. I experienced boredom and distraction plenty of times when trying to pray. I was spiritually helpless. That is, until I found help. My outlook on prayer, and the daily practice of it, changed when I learned the value of praying scripted, liturgical prayers.[1]

As a Christian growing up in Low Church evangelical and charismatic churches, I learned to value prayer for its originality and spontaneity. In these traditions, the highest form of prayer is prayer from the heart. Pastors and teachers taught me that Jesus gave us what we now call "the Lord's Prayer" as a pattern for us to learn how to pray from our hearts. According to these teachers, Jesus never intended us to pray those words as a scripted, memorized prayer. I believed this interpretation of prayer until, to my utter surprise, I discovered that the early church prayed the Lord's prayer as a prayer.

From the beginning, followers of Jesus memorized the Lord's Prayer and prayed it three times a day.[2] Some people object to reciting memorized prayers, arguing that praying written prayers cultivates a robotic, inauthentic spirituality. Granted, written prayers *can be* memorized and recited without any sense of life or attention to the presence of God. The temptation to recite heartless prayers is always present. But it's up to the person praying to determine whether to recite prayers lifelessly. A person full of faith and the Holy Spirit, giving full attention to the words of the Lord's Prayer, can pray it with the same intensity felt in a Pentecostal prayer meeting! Praying ancient prayers according to an ancient practice is one of the ways we avoid the arrogance of the modern world, where technologically advanced people value innovation, efficiency, and all things new and improved.

THE JESUS PRAYER

In addition to the Lord's Prayer and praying the Psalms, no other prayer is more ancient in the Christian tradition than the Jesus Prayer. Not only is this prayer rooted deeply within our history, but it's also the simplest way to go about centering Jesus in our prayers. The prayer itself is just ten words: *Lord Jesus Christ, Son of God, have mercy on me.*

This prayer has been central in Eastern Orthodox spirituality. For a long time in my Christian journey, I was ignorant of the experience of Orthodox Christians. I have two postgraduate degrees earned at two different seminaries—one Pentecostal and one Wesleyan—and neither exposed me to the theology and practices of the Orthodox

East. Pentecostalism and the Wesleyan-holiness movement belong to the Protestant tradition, which broke off from the Roman Catholic church. But the original church split was not between Catholics and Protestants. The first fracture in the history of the church was between Catholics in the West and the Orthodox in the East.

I love the body of Christ in all its various expressions. Now, I could fill volumes of books with my disagreements with various denominations, but I have chosen to live out Jesus' prayer that his followers would be one (John 17:11, 21). Instead of focusing on the practices and points of doctrine that divide us, I choose to focus on what I can learn from Christians who aren't like me. I've learned much about prayer from different traditions. The Baptists taught me to pray along with Scripture.[3] The charismatics taught me to pray with my spirit, not just my mind. The Anglicans taught me to pray with a prayer book. Benedictines within the Catholic tradition taught me to chant the Psalms. And the Orthodox have taught me to pray using the Jesus Prayer. Orthodox Christians have prayed this simple prayer for centuries. It has been a way for me to center my thoughts on King Jesus, the Lamb of God.

While Orthodox Christians made it popular, the prayer itself is rooted in the Gospels. Through a parable, Jesus revealed that prayer is a time and place for humility. He explained:

> Two men went up into the temple to pray, one a Pharisee and the other a tax collector. The Pharisee, standing by himself, prayed thus: "God, I thank you that I am not like other men, extortioners, unjust, adulterers, or even like this tax collector. I fast twice a week; I give tithes of all that I get." But the tax collector, standing far off, would not even lift up his eyes to heaven, but beat his breast, saying, "God, be merciful to me, a sinner!" I tell you, this man went down to his house justified, rather than the other. For everyone

who exalts himself will be humbled, but the one who
humbles himself will be exalted.
LUKE 18:10-14, ESV

The Pharisee boasting of his own greatness prayed a me-centered prayer. In contrast, the despised-but-humble tax collector prayed a mercy-centered prayer. The Jesus Prayer draws on the words of this tax collector. We are centering Jesus in our prayers when we pray a mercy-centered prayer reflecting the contrition of this sinner, who humbled himself in the presence of God.

Normally we pray in the name of Jesus by the power of the Spirit, addressing our prayers to God the Father. Jesus taught us to pray this way. Nevertheless we have no need to hesitate in addressing prayers to Jesus because he is "true God from true God," as we confess in the words of the Nicene Creed. Jesus is truly and fully God and therefore worthy to receive our prayers. We pray this particular prayer to Jesus. In so doing, we reflect a number of people in the Gospels who cried out to Jesus for mercy. For example, consider the story of Bartimaeus:

> They came to Jericho. And as he was leaving Jericho with
> his disciples and a great crowd, Bartimaeus, a blind beggar,
> the son of Timaeus, was sitting by the roadside. And when
> he heard that it was Jesus of Nazareth, he began to cry out
> and say, "Jesus, Son of David, *have mercy on me!*" And
> many rebuked him, telling him to be silent. But he cried out
> all the more, "Son of David, *have mercy on me!*"
> MARK 10:46-48, ESV, EMPHASIS ADDED[4]

While the Jesus Prayer finds its roots in Scripture, we learn how to pray this prayer from Eastern Orthodox Christians like bishop and theologian Kallistos Ware.[5] In his little book *The Jesus Prayer*, Ware described this prayer as a rope with four important strands:

1. the cry for mercy;
2. the discipline of repetition;
3. the quest for stillness; and
4. the veneration of the Holy Name.[6]

Let's look at each of these four strands as we seek to locate Jesus, the Lamb of God, in the center of our prayer life.

THE CRY FOR MERCY

This brief prayer contains a simple request: "Have mercy on me." This prayer for mercy isn't a plea for God to do something God doesn't want to do. God is not a grumpy, old curmudgeon with a scowl on his face, sitting angrily on a dusty throne in heaven. We don't need to cajole him into giving us mercy. God is like Jesus, who is the embodiment of mercy. This request for mercy in the Jesus Prayer is less about begging God for mercy and more about opening our hearts more fully to the God who is mercy. David praises the Lord, the God of Israel, saying, "Bless the LORD, O my soul, and all that is within me, bless his holy name. . . . The LORD is merciful and gracious, slow to anger and abounding in steadfast love" (Psalm 103:1, 8). Paul opens his second letter to the church in Corinth with these words, "Blessed be the God and Father of our Lord Jesus Christ, the Father of mercies and God of all comfort" (2 Corinthians 1:3, ESV). The God who is love shines bright with the light of mercy.

Orthodox teacher and author Frederica Mathewes-Green notes that we often forget our need for mercy. She writes:

> God doesn't need us to remind him to be merciful; he is merciful all the time, even when we don't ask. But unless we make a habit of asking for mercy, we forget that we *need* it. Ego builds a cardboard fortress that humility must, every day, tear down.[7]

Our ego inflated with self-aggrandizing pride does not create an impenetrable stone wall. Rather it fashions a flimsy cardboard fortress that clutters up our hearts. We tear this wall down with strength drawn from God's presence. As we work in prayer to keep Jesus at the center, we live under the waterfall of mercy, those mercies which are renewed every morning (Lamentations 3:22-23). When prayed regularly, the Jesus Prayer washes us clean from the pollution of selfish ambition and self-sufficiency. The mercy we seek heals us from our addiction to our own way of seeing things. This prayer subdues the autonomous thinking self's fight for control. Mercy flowing from the heart of God softens our hearts, reversing the effects of our stubborn pride, leaving us in a state of peace. We cannot experience God's peace without first experiencing God's mercy.

When do we need this mercy? Now! At least I need it now. I need God's mercy today and every day. We don't need a daily infusion of mercy because we are necessarily horrible, wretched creatures. Perhaps you have done bad things and you need pardon and healing from guilt and shame. If so, the Jesus Prayer is for you. But even if you haven't done things for which you feel guilty, you still need mercy today because of the gravitational pull toward the black hole of self-obsession. The request for mercy isn't a request for forgiveness for our wrongdoings as much as it is a request for help. When people approached Jesus and cried out "have mercy," they were not asking for forgiveness; they were asking for intervention. They were asking Jesus for help. David makes a similar request in the Psalms when he prays, "Have mercy on me, LORD, for I am in distress" (Psalm 31:9, NLT). I need mercy every day because some days I'm the prodigal son wasting the Father's inheritance and other days I'm the older brother refusing to join the party.

Sometimes we add the phrase "a sinner" to the end of the prayer. "Lord Jesus Christ, Son of God, have mercy on me, *a sinner*." I only do this once a day in morning prayer because my identity is rooted in my relation to Jesus: I am a person free from sin by God's grace. Repeatedly identifying myself as "a sinner" fails to emphasize my new identity. Nevertheless I recognize that at times I fail to reflect that image of love. For that I pray the Jesus Prayer spontaneously during the day.

The regular request for mercy drenches my heart in mercy, so when I experience stress or tragedy, what comes out is mercy. When I see the suffering of another, my reaction is to utter "Lord have mercy" because of years of praying this prayer. We cannot walk in the ways of Jesus without the mercy Jesus gives. As we pray for mercy, we are formed by it, so that when we are squeezed by the pressures of life, what comes out of our hearts and mouths is mercy, the same mercy we see in Jesus, our Passover Lamb. Jesus embodied the mercy of God in the way he taught and healed people, and we are walking in his footsteps.

THE VALUE OF REPETITION

In the Orthodox tradition the Jesus Prayer is prayed repeatedly, sometimes even one hundred times or more at a given time. I have learned the value of praying it that way. Inevitably people will ask about repeating this prayer over and over because of Jesus' warning about vain repetition when we pray. Let's take a closer look at Jesus' words, "When you pray, do not heap up empty phrases as the Gentiles do, for they think that they will be heard for their many words" (Matthew 6:7, ESV). The English translation "vain repetition" is found in the King James Version. It's the translation of a unique Greek word in the New Testament which means "to stammer" or "to babble," translated as "heap up empty phrases" in the NRSV.[8] The emphasis in Jesus' prohibition regarding prayer is not the repetition itself. On the contrary, Jesus' warning came as he was about to give his disciples a prayer that they would pray repeatedly. Repetition was not Jesus' concern, but rather doing so in a heartless, detached way. Presence of mind and attentiveness of heart are what Jesus is asking for.

The real issue Jesus addressed was the problem of using vain words, empty talk, and religious clichés that had lost their meaning but sounded impressive. Jesus wants to save us from hypocritical forms of prayer, the kinds that may look and sound eloquent but are just for show. Jesus again and again expressed his concern for the human heart and he cared about the deep connectivity human beings can experience in union with God. So the issue is not about repetition but about vanity. Jesus' desire for us is that we avoid the temptation to pray words without truly meaning them. He warns against using prayer to show off our spirituality—whether through never-ending repetition or spontaneous eloquence. That's where hypocrisy sets in.

The Jesus Prayer is anything but hypocritical. This ancient prayer has the potential to lead us into God's presence. The words of the Jesus Prayer aren't empty. By focusing on their meaning, we can more fully enter them and heed Jesus' warning. Consider the meaning of each word or phrase:

- *Lord*: The most significant word of our first confession, when we believe in our hearts and confess with our mouth that Jesus is Lord (Romans 10:9).

- *Jesus*: The holy name meaning "God saves" was shared by the angel who said, "You shall call his name Jesus, for he will save his people from their sins" (Matthew 1:21, ESV).

- *Christ*: The title given to Jesus meaning "king," specifically the Jewish king who would rule the nations.

- *Son of God*: The twofold descriptor of Jesus who is both the second person of the Trinity and the world's true political ruler.

- *Have mercy*: A request for the renewal of daily mercy.

- *On me*: One created in the image of God; an object of God's love and affection.

There is nothing empty about the words of this prayer. What can be shallow is us, the people praying it. We can be disinterested and unfocused when we try to settle into prayer. The real work of praying this prayer is providing intentionality every time we pray it. Mathewes-Green adds:

> The hard part is to pull together all your attention, though it kicks like a toddler, and focus it on the Lord, and then humbly ask for his mercy. Learning to actually mean the Jesus Prayer, from ever-deepening regions of your heart, is what makes the practice so challenging.[9]

This prayer is simple in its construction, but its practice is another matter. The benefits of this prayer make praying it continually worth it.

THE QUEST FOR STILLNESS

One of the most valuable effects of the Jesus Prayer is its ability to enable us to "pray without ceasing" (1 Thessalonians 5:17). Kallistos Ware encouraged people to pray at both "fixed times" and "free times," meaning we can pray this prayer whenever the words come to our minds and pass over our lips. While I pray this prayer specifically at three different times as a part of my "fixed" morning prayer, I also pray it freely throughout the day.

In his book *The Jesus Prayer*, Ware described how praying this prayer over and over allows the prayer to slip into our subconscious, so that it becomes part of us. He even describes Orthodox monks who pray this prayer hundreds of times a day, even waking themselves up at night praying the Jesus Prayer! While I've never woken myself up praying, I have begun to pray this prayer silently whenever I do wake up in the middle of the night and can't fall back asleep. It may only take me praying it three or four times before I am back to sleep. I can't explain it, but something about this prayer leads me into a place of stillness and peace.

Praying the Jesus Prayer is particularly helpful to prepare our hearts and minds for contemplative prayer, that is prayer without words. I'll admit that I haven't mastered contemplative prayer. Silence is still a challenge for me. Ware is helpful here:

> What matters in silence is not our external situation but our inner disposition. It is a matter, not of keeping our mouth shut, but of opening our heart to God. Silence, then, properly understood, implies not isolation but relationship. It denotes, in the context of worship, not rejection of the Other but acceptance. It is an attitude of receptivity and, above all, of *listening*.[10]

Sitting quietly in the presence of Jesus as an act of worship and prayer is the posture of passivity where we do not seek to get what we want but slow down and become still. In the raw vulnerability of silence, there is nothing to strive for. There is nothing to obtain, nothing to do other than to be loved by the God who dwells in silence. The Jesus Prayer has often helped me get to this place.

As Mathewes-Green noted above, the real work in praying this prayer is in bringing focus to each word in the prayer. Sometimes I follow the hesychastic prayer practice of the Orthodox and whisper each of the Jesus Prayers.[11] I do this by breathing in when I pray, *Lord Jesus Christ, Son of God* and then exhaling the words *have mercy on me*. Other times I simply whisper the entire ten-word prayer. I make sure I pray each word with humility and attention. I know for some

Christians these practices seem strange, but I can testify to their effectiveness. By the end of my time of praying the Jesus Prayer repeatedly, slowly, and intentionally, I feel unhurried and centered on Jesus. At that point I have entered a place of stillness and quiet and I'm ready to sit in silence, acknowledging God's presence.

The other form of praying that I have practiced is praying the Jesus Prayer slowly but removing a word or phrase each time I pray it, until I get to "Lord, have mercy." Praying this way has helped me maintain a sense of quietness. The prayer looks like this:

Lord Jesus Christ, Son of God, have mercy on me.
Lord Jesus Christ, Son of God, have mercy.
Lord Jesus Christ, have mercy.
Lord Jesus, have mercy.
Lord, have mercy.

Lord, have mercy. (12×)

Lord, have mercy.
Lord Jesus, have mercy.
Lord Jesus Christ, have mercy.
Lord Jesus Christ, Son of God, have mercy.
Lord Jesus Christ, Son of God, have mercy on me.
In the name of the Father, the Son, and the Holy Spirit. Amen.

After removing a word or a phrase each time until I get to "Lord, have mercy," I pray "Lord, have mercy" twelve times in a row slowly, pausing briefly after each time I pray it. Then I begin to add a word or phrase back in each line until I get to the full ten-word Jesus Prayer. The last time I pray it, I end the prayer with "in the name of the Father, the Son, and the Holy Spirit. Amen." This practice helps guide my heart and mind as I sit in silence.

THE VENERATION OF THE HOLY NAME

Finally we have come to the fourth and final strand of the Jesus Prayer and the most compelling reason we pray it. Ware instructs us to recognize the value of venerating the holy name of Jesus when we pray the Jesus Prayer. The word *veneration* means to show respect and honor. In a world where Jesus' name has become a popular profanity, those of us who love Jesus revere it in our prayers. Honoring and respecting the name of Jesus draws our attention to him. Respect in the Christian sense of the word is not something that can be demanded from us; it is something that we freely give. When we choose to honor or respect someone or something, we give it preeminence in our lives. We give it the power to form us in its image.

When we pray the Jesus Prayer, we are giving respect to Jesus, the Lamb of God; in doing so, we give Jesus the power to reshape us into his image by the Holy Spirit. In praying this prayer, we are becoming like Jesus and we are drawn deeper into a relationship with him. In the Orthodox tradition the purpose of praying this prayer is to come into union with Jesus. This is what Jesus wants. He told his disciples: "I am the vine; you are the branches. Whoever abides in me and I in him, he it is that bears much fruit, for apart from me you can do nothing" (John 15:5, ESV). Praying this prayer enables us to abide in him, and slowly, as we keep our eyes on Jesus, we find ourselves becoming more like him.

So how does one begin to enter this Jesus-centered prayer life? Start where you can. Pray this ten-word prayer early and often. You may not know much about breathing when you pray. That's okay. Find moments to incorporate this prayer into your life. Pray it before and after you spend time reading Scripture. Pray it between songs when you are worshiping with your local church. Pray it before you receive Communion. Pray it before you go to sleep at night. Pray it before you grab your phone in the morning. Pray it when you get dressed or when you get in the car. Pray it when you are in traffic. Pray it after you eat.

How you use this prayer is up to you, but find ways to pray it with great regularity. Then pay attention to how your heart is opening more and more to the presence of God, with Jesus at the center of it all.

DISCUSSION QUESTIONS

1. On a scale of one to ten, with one being "I'm a functional atheist" and ten being "I'm ready to join a monastery," how would you rate your prayer life?

2. What has been your experience with prayer? Has it been more free-flowing and spontaneous or structured and scripted? What are the pros and cons of each of these kinds of praying?

3. How does the request for mercy open us up to the mercy of God?

4. Why is the mercy of God necessary to experience the peace of God?

5. Does the idea of repetitive prayers make you feel intrigued or disinterested? Why?

6. Does stillness of body, mind, heart, and soul come easily to you, or is it a challenge? Why is it necessary for us to have moments of stillness throughout our day?

7. How does the proper respect for the name of Jesus keep Jesus centered in our hearts?

8. What is one thing you can do this week to incorporate the Jesus Prayer into your life?

A JESUS-CENTERED READING OF SCRIPTURE

Blessed Lord, who caused all holy Scriptures to be written
for our learning: Grant us so to hear them, read, mark, learn,
and inwardly digest them, that we may embrace and ever
hold fast the blessed hope of everlasting life, which you have
given us in our Savior Jesus Christ; who lives and reigns with
you and the Holy Spirit, one God, for ever and ever. Amen.

A COLLECT, PROPER 28,
THE BOOK OF COMMON PRAYER

I HAVE BEEN both a student and a teacher, a reader and an admirer, of the Bible for all my adult life. I started reading the Bible as a teenager, when I was taught how to have what my beloved Baptist mentors called a "quiet time." While my daily Bible reading has ebbed and flowed over the years, I am still reading our sacred Scriptures.

The Bible is—if I may be shockingly honest for a moment—a weird book. The names, the geography, the stories, the violence (*oh, the violence!*), the customs and interactions, the reports of what God says, the metaphors, and the poetry all pile up and look to the casual observer like a muddled mess of story, prophecy, wisdom, and letters. Yet the body of Christ flourishes when we commit our lives to these God-breathed words, which have been handed down to us from the church as our primary text. We find beauty, wonder and awe, and coherence when we allow Jesus to be our interpretive center.

Holy Christian Scripture sounds strange in our hearing because men moved by the Holy Spirit wrote those words thousands of years ago in different languages and in different historical contexts. It is *our* text, but while the Bible is written for our benefit—for our learning, growth, and formation into Christlikeness—it is not God's love letter written to us. As theologian Michael Bird notes, "Even though the Bible is *for us*, it was not written *to us*, nor was it written *about us*. . . . We have to grasp how strange the biblical world is before we can try to make it familiar to our own audiences."[1] The Bible contains the transformative power to shape our hearts and minds—when we approach it not as a collection of promises or principles but as a way to discover Jesus. When we treat it as a collection of inspirational sayings that we can easily apply to our lives, we both dishonor the sacred text and miss its primary purpose: to bear witness to Jesus, who is the living and reigning Word of God. To his Jewish brothers, Jesus said, "You search the scriptures because you think that in them you have eternal life; and it is they that testify on my behalf" (John 5:39). All Scripture is for us, but it is about Jesus.

The beauty of the Bible can be found in the attraction of its main character—King Jesus. When we read the Bible with Jesus at the center, it has the power and authority to renew our minds and hearts. It opens up to us as a formative text, showing us the mind and character of Jesus. Reading the Bible as a book about Jesus is how the church historically has read it. As Bird puts it: "To read Scripture as a Christian is to regard Scripture as finding its substance, coherence, and unity in Jesus Christ."[2]

Unfortunately, the more popular reading of the Bible, where readers find themselves at the center of the text, causes them to miss Jesus altogether or to invent an imaginary Jesus who looks and sounds a lot like the reader. We don't need a fake "Jesus" who is an amalgamation of all our hopes, dreams, and aspirations. We need a Jesus who, in the power of the Spirit, can lead us to understand all that has been written about him in Holy Scripture.

THE BIBLE SAYS IT, I BELIEVE IT, THAT SETTLES IT

When I came to faith in the late 1980s and early 1990s, Christian bumper stickers were in vogue. We hadn't seen the emergence of the plastic "Jesus fish" on the back of cars yet, but they would soon follow. These bumper stickers contained cheesy, pithy little slogans like:

"As long as there are tests, there will be prayer in schools."
"Not perfect, just forgiven."
"God is my copilot."
"My boss is a Jewish carpenter."
"Warning: In case of Rapture, this car will be unmanned."

And maybe my favorite . . .

"The Bible says it. I believe it. That settles it!"

I can laugh at these bumper stickers for the most part, but the last one stands out to me as less humorous and more serious, because that approach to Scripture can be a stumbling block. This bumper sticker could mean a lot of things, but generally it refers to an oversimplistic and hyperliteral interpretation of Scripture. But just like the bumper sticker, the Bible needs to be read with a bit more nuance and context to understand it in its fullness. Honestly, I don't think Christians who subscribe to the sentiment in that slogan actually believe it. Not that they don't believe in the Bible, but they don't believe in a strict literal interpretation of the Bible. Whenever people tell me that they don't interpret the Bible, they just "take it as it is," I always ask, "Why didn't you greet me with a holy kiss? I mean, Romans 16:16 is pretty clear that we should. So pucker up, Buttercup. It's kissing time!" Granted I am trying to inject a little humor to lower their defenses. But my hope is that we'll have an honest conversation about how we read—and more importantly, how we understand—Scripture.

In the fourth century, Hilary of Poitiers remarked, "Scripture is not in the reading, but in the understanding."[3] While we may be tempted to assume the Bible is easy to read and understand, we must reject such a temptation so that we honor the sacredness of Scripture. The cultural layers between us and the meaning behind the words create an interpretive web for us to navigate. For example, if we want to understand what Jesus meant in the Sermon on the Mount (Matthew 5–7), we have to start by admitting that we are reading an English translation of what Matthew wrote in Greek. But Jesus didn't speak Greek. He most likely spoke Aramaic. Furthermore, he had a mind shaped by prayer and Scriptures written in Hebrew. So when we read the Beatitudes (Matthew 5:1-12), we are reading what has been translated into English from Greek based on what was spoken in Aramaic from a Hebrew mind.

Clearly, we need help. Not only do we need help understanding the historical context of the words we read in Scripture, we also need an interpretative guide that can create cohesion between the many and varied books of the Bible. That way, we know not only what the text says but what it means. I have good news: Jesus is that guide!

The truth is that we all come to Scripture with a certain set of assumptions, biases, and interpretive constructs. We may or may not be aware of them, but we employ them to make sense of what we read. So, if we all have constructs that guide us in understanding what Scripture means, why not make Jesus our construct? Why not make Jesus the bias and the assumption? When we center Jesus in our reading of the Scripture, we find a faithful guide in all the peaks and valleys we come across.

If Jesus is going to be our guide, we need to define who Jesus is. In part, we know Jesus from the witness of the apostles, as recorded in Scripture. We also define Jesus the way the church has defined him since the fourth century by using the description given to us in the ancient creeds. According to them, he is "the only Son of God . . . true God from true God . . . of one Being with the Father . . . incarnate from the Virgin Mary."[4] Jesus is the one who was crucified, buried, and raised on the third day. He is the one who sits at the right hand of the Father, who will come to judge the living and the dead, "whose kingdom shall have no end."[5]

We place Jesus at the center of our Bible reading, in part, by looking for Jesus throughout the entire story the Bible tells. The Bible contains different kinds of writings—history, poetry, prophecy, proverbs, prayers, letters, and more, but the Bible tells a big, sweeping story from creation to new creation, from the garden of Eden to the new Jerusalem, and Jesus is the principal character.

Early Christians read the Bible believing the sacred Scriptures were revealing Jesus to the world. In the second century, Irenaeus wrote, "If anyone, therefore, reads the Scriptures with attention, he will find in them an account of Christ, and a foreshadowing of the new calling. . . . For Christ is the treasure which was hid in the field."[6] In the fifth century, Augustine exhorted Christians to pay careful attention to everything written in the Scripture so that they may discover their instructions and salvation in Jesus Christ. Augustine observed that when Jesus told the two disciples on the road to Emmaus about the necessity of a suffering Messiah, he did so by drawing on the ancient witness of Moses and the prophets. "Everything in the scriptures speaks of Christ," Augustine wrote, "but only to him who has ears. He opened their minds to understand the Scriptures, and so we should pray that he will open our own."[7]

READING IN THE EMMAUS WAY

By reading the Bible with a Jesus-centered lens, we allow Jesus to guide us to understand what we are reading. Jesus becomes both the central figure of the entire story of Scripture and our Rabbi, interpreting the Old Testament for us. When Jewish people work to understand what we Christians call the "Old Testament," they do so with the guidance of a teacher, a rabbi. Christians follow in this tradition when we allow Rabbi Jesus to guide us in understanding how the Law and Prophets reveal Jesus to us. Jesus himself said, "Do not think that I have come to abolish the law or the prophets; I have come not to abolish but to fulfill" (Matthew 5:17). Jesus fulfills what the Old Testament has to say about God's plan to rescue the world. Moses and the other biblical writers were writing about Jesus, though we can miss it at first glance.[8]

To see how Jesus is revealed in all Holy Scripture, we need a Christocentric reading of it, what Orthodox theologian Brad Jersak calls reading in the "Emmaus Way." In reading the Bible this way, we are not applying an artificial grid on top of the Bible and forcing it to say something it was never intended to say. Jersak remarks, "The *Emmaus Way* was never about changing what the Bible meant after the fact. Rather, it's an unveiling by the Spirit of God, who was already breathing through the words in anticipation of the incarnation."[9]

This way of reading Scripture has been given to us by Jesus as recorded in Luke's Gospel. Soon after Jesus was resurrected, he was walking incognito with two disciples who would have identified as Jesus followers. They were walking on the road that led from Jerusalem to the small village of Emmaus. Jesus jumped right into a conversation with these faithful disciples, but they didn't recognize him. He asked, "What are you discussing with each other while you walk along?" (Luke 24:17). They both looked sad and in sheer surprise one of them replied, "Are you the only stranger in Jerusalem who does not know the things that have taken place there in these days?" (Luke 24:18). Jesus continued to play coy and asked, "What things?" Without knowing it was Jesus to whom they were speaking, they told him what they knew. Jesus of Nazareth had come on the scene preaching, teaching, and performing miracles as a prophet of God. They had hoped Jesus would have been the one to redeem Israel, but he had been executed by the Romans.

I imagine at that moment these two disciples stopped on the road and grabbed Jesus by the arm to stop him, too, as they continued their account of what had happened. With a glimmer of renewed hope in their eyes, they told Jesus the surprising conclusion—some people are saying Jesus is alive! Then Jesus replied:

> "Oh, how foolish you are, and how slow of heart to believe all that the prophets have declared! Was it not necessary that the Messiah should suffer these things and then enter into his glory?" Then beginning with Moses and all the prophets, he interpreted to them the things about himself in all the scriptures.
> LUKE 24:25-27

Jesus would continue walking with these two disciples and share a meal with them, revealing himself further as he broke bread with them. The two were later reporting their experience to the other disciples when Jesus showed up out of nowhere in the middle of their conversation. The disciples thought they were looking at a ghost! Jesus calmed their fears and said, "These are my words that I spoke to you while I was still with you—that everything written about me in the law of Moses, the prophets, and the psalms must be fulfilled." He then proceeded to "[open] their minds to understand the scriptures" (Luke 24:44-45).

Jesus opened the Scriptures first to the two Jesus followers on the road to Emmaus to show them that Moses and all the prophets were writing about Jesus. Then he did the same thing for the other disciples. He gave them new eyes to see that the stories, prophecies, and prayers written in the Old Testament find their fulfillment in Jesus because as the embodiment of Israel's God, Jesus is what the story of Israel is all about.

Our prayer today is for Jesus to do the same thing for us. We need new eyes. We need Emmaus eyes. With these new eyes, the Holy Spirit empowers present-day followers of Jesus to see Jesus as the main character in the fascinating story Scripture tells. Once we begin to read and interpret Scripture this way, we cannot go back. We can no longer read the Old Testament without seeing the revelation of Jesus in those ancient words.

THE EMMAUS WAY IN ACTION

When we read the entire Bible in the Emmaus Way, we read Scripture in the way of Jesus. This is how Jesus read the Old Testament. And not only him but Paul and other New Testament writers, as well. Jesus dug deeply into the soil of the Hebrew Scriptures to unearth the hidden gems that shine with the brilliance of God's glory fulfilled in himself as he walked the earth. For example, Jesus delved into the account of Jonah swallowed up by that great fish to reveal his own resurrection from the dead. Jesus said:

> Just as Jonah was three days and three nights in the belly of the sea monster, so for three days and three nights the Son of Man will be in the heart of the earth. The people of Nineveh will rise up at the judgment with this generation and condemn it, because they repented at the proclamation of Jonah, and see, something greater than Jonah is here!
> MATTHEW 12:40-41

Jonah was a forerunner of the coming of King Jesus, who swallowed up death, defeating it for us through his death and resurrection. We find peace as our Bible reading is shaped by the Emmaus Way and Jesus our Rabbi reveals himself to us in Scripture.

Jesus did something similar in his conversation with the Jewish religious leader Nicodemus. Many Pharisees sparred with Jesus for his unconventional approach to faith, but Nicodemus was open to Jesus' messianic teaching. One night, while Jesus drew from a familiar story from Numbers 21:8-9, he said to Nicodemus: "Just as Moses lifted up the serpent in the wilderness, so must the Son of Man be lifted up, that whoever believes in him may have eternal life" (John 3:14-15). Jesus reflected on the scriptural image of a bronze snake on a pole and interpreted it in the Emmaus Way. Inspired by the Holy Spirit, Moses described a point in Israel's history when salvation and healing could be found by gazing on a bronze snake lifted for all to see. Little did Moses know that images like this one would find their fulfillment in King Jesus, the ruling Lamb of God. As Brad Jersak explains, "Christ and his gospel were embedded in the soil of the Old Testament by the Spirit. Now behold its telos in Jesus Christ."[10]

Like Jesus, the apostle Paul read the Old Testament in the Emmaus Way. In writing to the church in Corinth, Paul noted that before Jesus, the experiences of the ancient people of God were given as examples to guide us. Paul looked back at the Israelites wandering in the wilderness and saw Jesus in their midst. He wrote:

> I do not want you to be unaware, brothers and sisters, that our ancestors were all under the cloud, and all passed through the sea, and all were baptized into Moses in the cloud and in the sea, and all ate the same spiritual food, and all drank the same spiritual drink. For they drank from the spiritual rock that followed them, and the rock was Christ.
> 1 CORINTHIANS 10:1-4

Paul saw the rock in the wilderness in Exodus 17, and under its hard exterior, he found Jesus. We are centering Jesus in our Bible reading when we, like the apostle Paul, find Jesus tucked away in unexpected places in Holy Scripture.

Similarly, Peter learned the Emmaus Way of reading Scripture when Jesus appeared to him and the other disciples shortly after his resurrection. The apostle Peter carried on this practice by looking into the Old Testament to find Jesus there:

> He [Christ] went and preached to the spirits in prison— those who disobeyed God long ago when God waited patiently while Noah was building his boat. Only eight people were saved from drowning in that terrible flood. And that water is a picture of baptism, which now saves you, not by removing dirt from your body, but as a response to God from a clean conscience. It is effective because of the resurrection of Jesus Christ.
> 1 PETER 3:19-21, NLT

Peter looked back at the account of Noah and the Great Flood not as an account of God "determin[ing] to make an end of all flesh" (Genesis 6:13) but as a foreshadowing of God's work to open the door for all to find salvation by identifying with the crucified and risen Jesus through baptism.

THE FOUR SENSES OF SCRIPTURE

In addition to the Emmaus Way of reading Scripture, with Jesus as the center, I want to introduce you to four ways of understanding Scripture. These four senses fit well with what we've already covered; in fact, the Emmaus Way is an example of one of these senses. Each one helps us discover surprising insights that can both deepen and expand our reading. And to introduce you to these four approaches to understanding the Bible, I want to acquaint you with another theologian—Thomas Aquinas.

Perhaps no other figure besides Augustine has been as influential in Western Christianity. As a thirteenth-century Italian-born son of a nobleman, Aquinas devoted his life to God through prayer, study, and careful reflection. His massively influential work, *Summa Theologica*, drew on Greek philosophy, particularly from Aristotle, to consider the knowledge of God and God's work on earth. He has been revered as a saint and a "Doctor of the Church" because of this theological contribution to the faith, notably in apologetics and moral theology. Aquinas helps us read the Bible in the Emmaus Way with Jesus at the center. In his *Summa Theologica*, Aquinas describes four senses or meanings of Scripture:

- historical (literal);
- allegorical (symbolic);
- ethical (moral); and
- mystical (anagogical).[11]

Aquinas argued for reading Scripture with multiple meanings because God is at work in multiple ways, revealing to us what God wants us to know, not only by the words themselves but by what the words point us to, which ultimately is Jesus.

We all interpret the meaning of words, whether they are spoken or written. Deriving meaning from words is how language works. We use words in different ways to communicate different things. Sometimes we use them in a literal sense. For example, "Can you pour me a cup of coffee?" Sometimes we use words in a figurative sense, like "I'm feeling under the weather today." The more familiar we are with a certain culture, the quicker and more intuitively we identify figurative language and interpret its meaning in that context. When it comes to an ancient collection of writing like Holy Scripture, however, interpretation can be a bit more difficult.

For Aquinas, interpretation of Scripture is not divided into literal and figurative but literal and "spiritual," with the spiritual sense including allegorical, ethical, and mystical meanings. The historical meaning (the first sense) grounds our interpretation within the historical and cultural context of the original hearers. We start with the historical meaning so we have a grasp on what the text *meant*. But today, as followers of Jesus living thousands of years after those original hearers, we want to know what any given text *means* for us. These meanings come from the final three senses offered by Aquinas. And they demonstrate why we can't simply rest on a literal interpretation of Scripture alone.

The allegorical or symbolic meaning asks followers of Jesus to search for Jesus in any text of Scripture—reading in the Emmaus Way. The ethical or moral meaning asks what a certain Scripture passage calls us to do as followers of Jesus. Finally, the mystical, or anagogical,[12] meaning of Scripture draws our hearts toward God.

These four senses offer a helpful guide in reading all Scripture with Jesus, the Lamb of God, at the center. These senses offer us four questions to ask as we are studying and reading the Bible on our own or with other followers of Jesus:

- *Historical*: What does this text say within its cultural context?
- *Allegorical*: How does this text reveal Jesus to us?
- *Ethical*: What does this text call us to do as followers of Jesus?
- *Mystical*: How does this text draw us near to God?

For example, let's return to the playful question I ask people when they tell me that they "take the Bible as it is"—"Why didn't you greet me with a holy kiss?" Their approach is grounded in only one meaning of Scripture, the literal, historical sense. Here is how I use the questions above to read and interpret Romans 16:16, "Greet one another with a holy kiss," in a Jesus-focused way.

First, what does this text say within its cultural context (the historical sense)? I understand from historians that first-century Christians would kiss each other on the cheek as a part of worship. Some cultures still carry on that practice. I remember being an awkward eighteen-year-old in a church in northern Mexico when they greeted their neighbors not with a handshake but with a literal kiss!

Second, how does this text reveal Jesus to us (the allegorical sense)? I see within that kiss the Lord Jesus, where "righteousness and peace . . . kiss each other" (Psalm 85:10). For us, Jesus is the righteousness of God and the peace of God.

Third, what does this text call us to do as followers of Jesus (the ethical sense)? I see in Paul's exhortation a call to love one another not with a cheap, surface, sentimental love but with deep brotherly affection.

Finally, how does this text draw us near to God (the mystical sense)? The call to kiss draws us near to God in an intimate embrace where we know and are known, where we love and are loved by God.

These four senses, and the questions they prompt, offer us a helpful tool in keeping Jesus foremost in our Scripture reading. They provide a tremendous resource in making sense of some of the trickier-to-interpret parts of the Bible, particularly some of the hyperviolent Old Testament passages. The four senses help us see how the Bible, the written word of God, leads us to Jesus, the living Word of God, whom we look to for healing, redemption, and salvation. After all, Jesus—not the Bible—is the Savior of the world. Devoting ourselves to reading the Bible daily on our own and listening to Scripture read aloud in worship gatherings are essential Christian practices. We derive the most benefit from Scripture when we allow the Spirit behind the text to guide us to Jesus in the text.

Reading Scripture in this fourfold way has increased the joy I experience in my own daily Bible reading, which has dramatically increased in the last few years as I have become more consistent in this practice.[13] In my personal reading of Scripture, I am much more attuned to looking for Jesus in the Old Testament. When I come across a passage that doesn't look much like Jesus, I ask myself questions like *Where do I see Jesus here? What is this text calling me to do or not do as a follower of Jesus? How does this text, which seems confusing, draw me closer to the heart of God?* Sometimes an answer comes to me and sometimes it does not. In those moments where I don't sense an answer to a puzzling text, I simply move on.

Reading in the Emmaus Way and opening our imagination to the other senses of Scripture moves us from a limited, bumper-sticker kind of Christianity into a richer and deeper faith because we are allowed to see Scripture in its fullness. Centering Jesus as the Lamb in our reading of Scripture prevents us from placing ourselves in the center of the story the Bible is telling. It also prevents violent images in parts of the Hebrew Scriptures from becoming normative in our lives. With the Lamb at the center of our reading, we discover that we do not pick up the sword because we are following the Lamb, who moved through the world with love and compassion.

DISCUSSION QUESTIONS

1. Do you find Bible reading to be a challenge, a delight, or something else?

2. What kind of Bible reading plans or strategies have you used in the past?

3. Why is it problematic to attempt to read every verse of Scripture in a literal way, with a literal application to your life?

4. Describe in your own words what it means for Jesus to be our Rabbi, leading and teaching us through the entirety of Scripture.

5. Consider the four senses of Scripture: historical, allegorical, ethical, and mystical. Which sense, or meaning, is your heart most drawn toward?

6. What resources can we use to understand the historical meaning of Scripture?

7. What do you do when you read a particular passage in the Bible and struggle to see Jesus in it?

8. What is one new practice you can add to your Bible reading to keep your focus on Jesus?

THE SPIRIT POINTS
US TO JESUS

O God, because without you we are not able to please
you, mercifully grant that your Holy Spirit may in all things
direct and rule our hearts; through Jesus Christ our Lord,
who lives and reigns with you and the Holy Spirit, one God,
now and for ever. Amen.

A COLLECT, PROPER 19,
THE BOOK OF COMMON PRAYER

THE SLOGAN "I'M SPIRITUAL but not religious" remains popular among many people throughout North America. In 2017 the Pew Research Center revealed the results of a study showing that 27 percent of American adults define themselves as spiritual but not religious, which is up by 8 percent from five years prior. Study respondents who claimed to be both religious and spiritual (48 percent) are down from 59 percent in 2012.[1] I suppose these trends toward spirituality and away from religion have only continued in our post-pandemic world. In a culture dominated by a way of knowing limited to the five physical senses, I appreciate that spirituality has its foot in the cultural door. I'm grateful for all that empirical knowledge has done for medical science, but it has its limitations. Empirical knowledge can help us know which medications can combat which diseases, but it cannot tell us why we should care for sick people in the first place. Knowing through observation and testing can reveal how the human body functions, but this kind of knowledge cannot show us the ultimate purpose of humanity.

Spirituality offers the kind of transcendence that makes it possible to discover purpose and meaning. Yet while spirituality is on the rise in the United States, institutional religion continues to decrease in popularity.[2] It appears that Americans are growing in their openness to spirituality, but not the kind of spirituality offered in organized religion, not the kind of spirituality offered by the body of Christ. I rejoice in the rise of spirituality because it opens the door for the gospel of King Jesus. Jesus shows us how to be human beings fully alive both physically and spiritually. The God of creation, who is perfect love, has come to us in the person of Jesus Christ to rid the world of evil, sin, and death through his life, death, resurrection, and ascension. Remaining Christian in the historical sense requires a spirituality that is grounded in the person and teachings of Jesus and sustained by the church. A general disposition toward generic spirituality isn't going to lead people to Jesus. We need a *Jesus-centered* spirituality.

It's not surprising that more and more people are abandoning the label "religious" because Christian institutions from the Roman Catholic church to evangelical megachurches have exhibited scandalous behavior, including toxic leadership, sexual abuse, and the covering up of those things by people who knew what was happening but did nothing to stop the offender or prevent the offense from happening again. Scot McKnight and Laura Barringer have argued that harmful churches that wound people not only have toxic leaders but also have toxic cultures.[3] Churches with unhealthy cultures soil the reputation of religion and send people looking for a spirituality outside the church that will allow them to connect to something beyond themselves. If my experience as a pastor has proven anything, it has shown me that this trend will only continue.

I understand the appeal of spirituality because God has made us hybrid creatures: not all body, not all materiality, but body *and soul*. We are people of the earth, people of the soil, but we are also people of heaven, people of the Spirit. God formed humanity as living creatures from the dust of the earth and then breathed into them the breath of life. This breath is the breath of heaven, the *ruach*, the Hebrew word for breath or spirit. The longing for spiritual things persists among us modern people because we were created for more than what this physical world can provide. The ache for transcendence, the desire to go beyond ourselves and connect our lives to something bigger than ourselves, is deeply human.

I do understand the decline of religion in general, and the Christian religion in particular, in North America. Not only have toxic leadership failures and sexual abuse scandals called into question the legitimacy of religion, but the rapidly growing normalcy of digital forms of communication, learning, and experience have empowered the autonomous thinking self to be the curator of spiritual truth. For some people the rationale is *Why should I go to church when I can go online to get all I need to be a moral and spiritual person?* We are witnessing the full-blown flowering of Enlightenment ideals, on which American culture and Western civilization is built. The rugged individualist has a smartphone, a smart TV, a laptop, a Wi-Fi connection, and a diminishing need for professional religious people.

Modern Americans assume the lone educated individual can cobble together a custom-made "Christian" spirituality drawn from an assortment of Christian language, texts, and practices. The use of Christian images and ideas makes a homemade spirituality look Christian, but it lacks the substance of the historic Christian tradition. And a modern, individualistic spirituality without the form and shape of the great Christian tradition can quickly begin to look somewhat less Christlike. Theologian and biblical scholar N. T. Wright describes this kind of spirituality as a broken signpost, where individuals look within to cultivate a "spiritual life" based on one's desires and inclinations.[4] Many modern people want to disregard the structure of religion because while they may be open to something transcendent, they want to define the value of transcendent, spiritual experiences on their own terms. They do not want religion telling them how to make sense of their experience of the divine.

Religion has its place in the modern world because as James K. A. Smith has argued, we are creatures with instincts toward ritual. Smith writes, "To be human is to be a liturgical animal, a creature whose loves are shaped by our worship. And worship isn't optional."[5] Jesus certainly critiqued bad religion. He saved his sharpest critique for *hypocritical* religion, *self-righteous* religion, and *oppressive* religion, but he continued the practice of first-century Jewish religion. He participated in synagogue worship on the Sabbath and in the annual Jewish feasts. As followers of Jesus, we experience a spirituality centered on Jesus, one not untethered from religion. The shape of our spirituality is formed by the practice of the Christian religion, with a devotion to its sacred Scriptures, prayers, creeds, and forms of worship. We are liturgical animals who practice the Christian religion, and we are equally spirit-infused animals who practice the art of Christian spirituality. What makes Christian spirituality *spiritual* is that it is a lived experience of the Holy Spirit. What makes Christian spirituality *Christian* is that it is intentionally focused on Jesus. Let's look at how the Holy Spirit, as the third person of the Trinity, empowers us on our journey of centering Jesus.

GOD'S LIFE-GIVING PRESENCE

The words *spirituality* and *spiritual* can become slippery because people use them in so many different ways. People in popular culture use the term *spiritual* often to mean "immaterial," that is, those realities that exist outside the reach of what can be seen, heard, or touched.

Christians often use the adjective *spiritual* to describe something associated with their relationship with God, for example, spiritual growth, spiritual disciplines, and spiritual formation. Going to church is "spiritual," as are prayer and Bible reading. "Spiritual Christians"—or better yet, "super-spiritual Christians"—are those who invest a large portion of their time and energy in spiritual activities. In this context, "spiritual" means what we do with our "spirits."

This use of the word *spiritual* isn't exactly how the word is used in Scripture, however. In the New Testament, the apostle Paul almost exclusively used the word *spiritual*, and he used it in a specific way. For Paul, spiritual is "that which belongs to, or pertains to, the Spirit."[6] New Testament scholar Gordon Fee offers this linguistic warning:

> The small case "spiritual" probably should be eliminated from our vocabulary, when it comes to this word in the Pauline corpus. . . . In fact, there is not a single instance in Paul where this word refers to the human "spirit" and has to do with "spiritual life," as this word is most often understood in modern English. For Paul it is an adjective that primarily refers to the Spirit of God.[7]

When we look to Paul's letters to guide our understanding of Christian spirituality, we can avoid the anachronistic temptation to read our modern understanding of spirituality into the New Testament. The kind of spirituality Paul writes about is a spirituality bathed in the life of God the Holy Spirit. The word *spiritual* describes our connectivity to the Spirit. To be a spiritual person according to Paul is to be a person who walks in the Holy Spirit.

In Paul's detailed description of the bodily resurrection that awaits us at the end of the age, he describes the bodies we will receive as spiritual bodies (1 Corinthians 15:44). Paul described these future bodies in the context of the essential Christian belief in the resurrection of Jesus from the dead. The lynchpin of the Christian faith is the literal, historical, and physical resurrection of Jesus who rose, not as a nonmaterial spirit but as a real flesh-and-blood human being so that he might become, as Paul described it, "a life-giving spirit" (1 Corinthians 15:45). Jesus' resurrection wasn't nonmaterial, and neither shall ours be. God raised Jesus from the dead by the Holy Spirit (Romans 8:11). Jesus became a life-giving spirit as a real flesh-and-blood human being. When we are raised to eternal life and immortality by the Holy Spirit, we shall receive a spiritual body, a real human body animated by the Spirit.

To be a spiritual person and to explore Christian spirituality from a historic Christian point of view is to be a person baptized in, and filled with, God's Spirit. Our spiritual life is not measured by our activity or our knowledge, but by our proximity and response to God the Holy Spirit, the Giver of Life. Our baptism in the Holy Spirit is by nature an experiential plunge into the life of God, which transcends our knowledge of God and gives us a renewed focus on Jesus, the Lamb of God. Pentecostal and non-Pentecostal Christians disagree on the exact nature of this experience, but determining when one experiences Spirit baptism is of less importance to me. I'm more interested in the daily lived experience of the Holy Spirit by all those who are following Jesus. Perhaps we can agree to some degree with the words of Roman Catholic preacher Raniero Cantalamessa:

> Not only through the sacrament of baptism that he instituted, but throughout the whole of his work, Jesus "baptizes in the Holy Spirit." His entire messianic mission consists in pouring out the Holy Spirit upon the world. The baptism in the Holy Spirit . . . is one of the ways in which the risen Jesus continues his essential work, which is to baptize all of humankind "in the Spirit."[8]

In a beautiful act of unity and symmetry, Jesus baptizes us in the Holy Spirit so that the Holy Spirit might glorify Jesus, taking what is his and making it known to us. Jesus said, "When the Spirit of truth comes, he will guide you into all the truth, for he will not speak on his own authority, but whatever he hears he will speak, and he will declare to you the things that are to come. *He will glorify me*, for he will take what is mine and declare it to you" (John 16:13-14, ESV, emphasis added). In this regard, the Holy Spirit appears to take a back seat to Jesus and the Father by choosing to direct our attention to Jesus. The Spirit is fully God and fully present in all the actions of the Trinity, but he too easily becomes, in the words of Francis Chan, "the forgotten God."[9] We practice a Spirit-baptized spirituality when we openly participate with this work of the Spirit to keep our focus on Jesus.

THE OPENNESS OF THE TRINITY

We who identify with the Christian faith have a striking and unique way of describing the one God we worship. We are followers of Jesus. He has always been at the center of our faith. We believe Jesus is God, the "visible image of the invisible God" (Colossians 1:15, NLT) in whom "lives all the fullness of God in a human body" (Colossians 2:9, NLT). As a human being, Jesus perfectly shows us what God is like, because Jesus *is* God. But our unique understanding of God doesn't end there because Jesus called God his Father. In fact, Jesus taught us to pray using the words *Our Father . . .* (Matthew 6:9). So if Jesus is God and he prayed to God whom he called Father, then who *is* God if there is only one God? Hold on for a moment because the complexity continues.

Jesus also taught us that after him would come the "Spirit of truth," whom Jesus called "the Advocate," who would come from the Father to testify on the Son's behalf (John 15:26). Jesus describes this Advocate, the Holy Spirit, in ways that sound like God too. The unique picture of the Christian God looks something like this:

God the Father sends Jesus, the Son of God, so that we can see the heart of the Father. In Jesus the invisible God has been made visible. Through the Son, the Father sends the Holy Spirit to point us back to Jesus. These three work together in beautiful harmony as the one true living God. The word Christians have used for seventeen hundred years to talk about this complex image of God is *Trinity*.

The Trinity isn't a mathematical problem to be solved but a divine mystery to be explored. We believe God is one in God's divine nature, but this one God has been revealed in three distinct persons, a dynamic community of love. God is love not in theory or abstraction. God is love in a holy and eternal relationship. God is love without being selfish. God is love as revealed in the love expressed among the Father, Son, and Holy Spirit.

Since the fourth century, it has been popular for Christians to describe this love-in-relationship in a way that identifies the Holy Spirit as the love shared between the Father and the Son. As it has been understood, God the Father is the Lover. Jesus is the Beloved. The Holy Spirit is the mutual love they share.[10] In this model of the Trinity, the Father and Son are described in personal, familial terms and the Holy Spirit is described in a more abstract way.[11]

This interpretation of the Trinity is helpful, but all human descriptions of the Holy Trinity break down at some point. It is true that the Holy Spirit is love because God is love and the Holy Spirit is God. Nevertheless the "lover, beloved, and love shared" characterization obscures the full personhood of the Spirit. The Holy Spirit as mutual love reduces the third person of the Trinity to something like "the Force" in the *Star Wars* universe. Whereas the historic Christian position has been to describe the Holy Spirit as "the Lord, the giver of life."[12]

A better model of the Trinity was given to us by Irenaeus in the second century. He described humankind being made by the two hands of the Father.[13] Irenaeus described humanity as God's handiwork fashioned after the likeness of God's own Son and the two hands accomplishing this task are the Son and the Spirit. This admittedly imperfect picture of the Trinity reveals a God who is open and at work. The Spirit isn't the bond that seals up the Trinity; rather, the Spirit is the hand that gestures to the world to draw near and be embraced by the God of pure love. The "Spirit as mutual love" view of the Trinity not only obscures the full personhood of the Spirit, it also minimizes the mission and work of the Holy Spirit, who, along with the bride, invites us into the life of God centered on Jesus. Near the end of Revelation, we read:

> The Spirit and the bride say, "Come."
> And let everyone who hears say, "Come."
> And let everyone who is thirsty come.
> Let anyone who wishes take the water of life as a gift.
> REVELATION 22:17

The Spirit speaks and motions to everyone who hears to come and experience the gift of life. God the Holy Spirit isn't only the closed loop of love exchanged by the Father and the Son because that image closes the circle of Trinitarian life. Rather the Spirit is the hospitable, open love of God beckoning us to find a new home, a new life, in the very life of God.

The Holy Spirit was the means by which life came into existence, and the Spirit empowered Jesus in his missional life of proclaiming and demonstrating God's Kingdom. God the Father poured this same Spirit on the church, breathing the breath of life into a community that might carry forth the message and ministry of Jesus. According to British theologian Colin Gunton:

> The third person of the Trinity is the one whose function
> is to make the love of God a love that is opened towards
> that which is not itself, to perfect it in otherness. Because

God is not in himself a closed circle but is essentially
the relatedness of community, there is within his eternal
being that which freely and in love creates, reconciles and
redeems that which is not himself.[14]

The Spirit reconciles and redeems us by forming us and conforming us into the lamblike image of Jesus as the Spirit directs our full attention to Jesus. The Holy Spirit is both the hand of God motioning for us to enter the love of the Holy Trinity and the finger of God pointing us to Jesus. The ninth-century hymn "Come, Creator Spirit" (Latin: *Veni Creator Spiritus*) that has been used in Catholic and Protestant worship speaks of the Spirit as the finger of God.

Come, Creator Spirit,
visit the minds of those who are yours;
fill with heavenly grace
the hearts that you have made.

You who are named the Paraclete,
gift of God most high,
living fountain, fire, love
and anointing for the soul.

You are sevenfold in your gifts,
you are finger of God's right hand.[15]

The same hand that gestures for us to come is the finger of God directing our attention to the Lamb of God.

A SPOTLIGHT ON JESUS

To be intentionally Trinitarian, to be a gathering of people who find a home in the life of the Father, Son, and Holy Spirit, is to be intentionally Jesus centered because as we gaze on the beauty of the Trinity, the spotlight is on Jesus. The Father sent the Son to make known the Father's heart to us (John 1:18), and through the Son the Father sent the Spirit, that he might take what belongs to Jesus and make it known to us (John 16:14). In the end, the mutually submissive and self-giving members of the Trinity continually point to Jesus. Nowhere in the Gospels do we see this more clearly than in the account of Jesus' baptism, which Matthew captures with these words:

> When Jesus had been baptized, just as he came up from the water, suddenly the heavens were opened to him and he saw the Spirit of God descending like a dove and alighting on him. And a voice from heaven said, "This is my Son, the Beloved, with whom I am well pleased."
> MATTHEW 3:16-17

Scripture's description of the dove illustrates the Holy Spirit's quiet emphasis on Jesus. Some modern English translations describe the Spirit descending like a dove and "settling" on him.[16] The NRSV uses the phrase "alighting on him," which creates a delightful image. In English *alighting* is used to describe the action of a bird descending and landing on a branch. It's such a simple, delicate, and beautiful act worth observing: at Jesus' baptism the Holy Spirit quietly comes to rest on Jesus' shoulder. The Spirit doesn't require fanfare or acclaim. When the Spirit descends like a dove, the angels don't sing. People don't gather to observe. Similarly, when God the Father speaks, the words direct our gaze not to the dove but to Jesus, the one the Father loves. God the Holy Spirit gracefully rests on Jesus to shine the light on the one who John the Baptist called the Lamb of God (John 1:29).

In some ways the Holy Spirit functions as the behind-the-scenes member of the Trinity, empowering the church to see more clearly the brightness and beauty of the Lamb of God, who leads us to the good life. In a distracting world filled with competing images of the good life, the Holy Spirit empowers us to stay focused on Jesus to experience eternal life. We are running a race in tandem with the Lamb of God, which requires endurance and a steady pace. The Holy Spirit helps us run. We cannot be encumbered by sins that might trip us up, preventing us from reaching the finish line. The Holy Spirit helps us shed those sins. We run this race by "looking to Jesus the pioneer and perfecter of our faith" (Hebrews 12:2). The Spirit at times gently turns our faces that we might look full into the face of Jesus. It's the Spirit who enables us to experience the words of the old hymn:

> Turn your eyes upon Jesus,
> Look full in His wonderful face,
> And the things of earth will grow strangely dim,
> In the light of His glory and grace.[17]

The Holy Spirit strengthens us in our work of centering Jesus, so that in running "the race that is set before us" (Hebrews 12:2), we may be fueled by love, which is the substance of all Christian spirituality. In this way, we open ourselves to words of Paul's prayer, "I pray that you may have the power to comprehend, with all the saints, what is the breadth and length and height and depth, and to know the love of Christ that surpasses knowledge, so that you may be filled with all the fullness of God" (Ephesians 3:18-19). In the depth of that ocean, we find our identity and purpose. "Contemporary spirituality," according to pastor and theologian Eugene Peterson, "desperately needs focus, precision, and roots: focus on Christ, precision in the Scriptures, and roots in a healthy tradition."[18] Christian spirituality causes our lives to fall into orbit around Christ. He is our focus. Not the Jesus we create in our imaginations, but the Jesus proclaimed to us in all Holy Scripture.

In heeding Peterson's advice, we root ourselves in the great

Christian tradition, particularly the traditions related to Scripture reading and prayer. The Spirit sustains us in our life of prayer, often "with groanings too deep for words" (Romans 8:26, ESV). When our attention begins to run wild in prayer, God the Holy Spirit gently draws our attention back to Jesus. The Spirit also comes alongside us as we open Holy Scripture. We work with precision to saturate our hearts and imaginations in the grand story unfolding in Scripture, a story which casts Jesus as the main character. The Spirit who inspired the text is the same Spirit who can lead us to see Jesus in the text. He can guide us as we look for what any passage is calling us to do as followers of Jesus. Furthermore, the Spirit makes real our direct encounter with God through Bible reading. We devote ourselves to Scripture and prayer so we can focus on Jesus. In its essence Christian spirituality is a Spirit-born attentiveness to the work of God in and through Jesus. Our responsibility is to cooperate with the Spirit in the practices we keep and in the way we prioritize our lives. We will be more attentive to Jesus when we devote ourselves to daily prayer, weekly worship, and regular times of Bible reading.

DISCUSSION QUESTIONS

1. Has there been a time in your life when you would have called yourself a "spiritual person" or a "religious person"? If so, how would you have described yourself then? If not, how have you heard others who identify as "spiritual" or "religious" describe themselves?

2. Why do you think so many people are abandoning organized religion?

3. Why is spirituality without a religious context so difficult to define?

4. What has your experience with the Holy Spirit been like?

5. What are the differences between the Holy Spirit as the love between the Father and the Son and the Holy Spirit as the hand of God reaching out to us?

6. What does the Holy Spirit do to direct our attention to Jesus?

7. What would it look like for us to practice a Jesus-centered spirituality together?

8. What is one thing you can do to open yourself more fully to the Holy Spirit?

CHRISTIAN VIRTUES

OUR AGE OF disinformation and stubborn pragmatism is slowly eroding our sense of virtue. Far too many people meet ethical challenges by relying on how they feel, whatever they can glean from social media, and pop "wisdom" from a sixty-second Google search. Whereas people with sincere moral character were once generally regarded as the ideal throughout Western civilization, modern Americans don't seem to value such people as much as they value those who produce results. Character has been set aside in favor of productivity. I suppose people are asking themselves *What's the value of being kind, merciful, and peaceable if I cannot get the job done?*

I have observed the shift in moral decision making from character to consequences within various forms of evangelicalism. I continue to see a growing emphasis in evaluating ethical dilemmas based on outcomes. Certainly we do factor consequences into how we make moral decisions. I have done that in teaching my children right and wrong, by explaining things like "We do not lie because lying breaks trust." Consequences have a necessary role in how we think about ethics, but if they become our primary focus, we drift into a pragmatic form of moral decision making, where the emphasis is no longer on people but production. If the question becomes *What will be the outcome of this decision?* we can justify meanness or cruelty to produce the outcomes we desire.

Injustice thrives when people become secondary to productivity. We shouldn't lose sight of the consequences of our moral decisions, but we need to keep our focus on how those consequences affect the object of God's love and attention—humanity, in all our diversity and splendor. Moreover, as followers of Jesus, we must renew our focus on Christian virtues, so that we become people who exhibit the character of Christ regardless of the consequences. Becoming a virtuous person does not ensure that we will always be well-liked or successful according to modern definitions of *success*. But it does mean becoming the image bearers of God that we were created to be.

Sadly the decline of virtue ethics in favor of consequentialism has seeped into the church. We can find a remnant keeping the virtue torch burning bright, but their number is dwindling. The cracks in our moral foundation continue to multiply with every announcement of another Christian leader who has done very un-Christian things. Without a foundation of moral virtues, we are left with the shifting sands of pride, popular opinion, and power to get people to do what we want, none of which have anything to do with the Kingdom of God. Followers of Jesus desperately need a renewal of the ancient Christian virtues of faith, hope, and love. These three virtues given to us by God shape our moral life as we follow the Lamb, serving as the foundation of all other virtues. They form a moral compass embedded deep within our hearts, giving us the instincts to walk in the way of Jesus.

Theologian and former Archbishop of Canterbury Rowan Williams has wisely called for a renewal of Jesus-focused virtues:

> In the midst of the anxieties and obsessions that characterize our age, we might come to rediscover the three "theological virtues" of faith and hope and love. We rediscover them as we discover that relationship which makes us whole, that relationship with the unconditional presence and witness, absolution and affirmation that belong to God. We discover all this, in short, in relation to the God of the Gospels, the God of Jesus, the God Jesus is.[1]

We turn our attention to faith, hope, and love as foundational virtues, keeping Jesus as the Lamb of God at the center of each one. As we grow in virtue, we become faithful, hopeful, and loving people who choose the good and the beautiful regardless of the outcomes of such choices. In the next few chapters we will take an in-depth look at the nature of faith. This deep dive will lead us to consider the virtue of hope, whereby our ethical orientation is set by our vision of God's future. Finally we will consider love as the centerpiece of all virtues and look at a number of habits that allow us to grow in love.

THE FOUR SIDES OF FAITH

Almighty and everlasting God, increase in us the gifts of
faith, hope, and charity; and, that we may obtain what you
promise, make us love what you command; through Jesus
Christ our Lord, who lives and reigns with you and the Holy
Spirit, one God, for ever and ever. Amen.

A COLLECT, PROPER 25,
THE BOOK OF COMMON PRAYER

BEFORE WE EXPLORE FAITH, the first of the theological virtues, let's slow down a moment and sketch a working definition of
virtue. If virtue has indeed been overtaken by other options as the way
we determine right and wrong, then we need a clear understanding of
virtue, so we know what we are called to pursue as followers of Jesus.

Virtue is a quality of the heart. Paul exhorted the church to think
on a number of things, including virtue. He wrote, "Finally, brothers,
whatever is true, whatever is honorable, whatever is just, whatever
is pure, whatever is lovely, whatever is commendable, if there is any
excellence, if there is anything worthy of praise, think about these
things" (Philippians 4:8, ESV, emphasis added). The English word
translated "excellence" is *aretē*, meaning virtue or moral excellence.

Virtue is the moral content of a person's character. Virtue isn't merely knowing what is good and right and then considering whether or not to do what is good and right. Rather, virtue is being a good and right *person*. When faced with a moral dilemma, the virtuous person instinctively chooses the moral good. We can possess virtue, but not in the same way we possess knowledge. I love sports, but possessing the technical knowledge about a given sport isn't the same thing as possessing athleticism. I can explain the game of football with some detail, but I don't possess the agility, fitness, strength, or speed to play the game competitively. Athleticism is to professional football players what virtues are to the mature human soul. Ethicist Joseph Kotva writes:

> The virtues simply are those states of character acquired over time that contribute to the realization of the human good. The virtues involve both the intellect and the will, the rational and affective parts of the self. They also involve tendencies, dispositions, and capabilities.[1]

In a very cyclical way, virtue is a state of being that develops from a certain kind of doing, so that the way we live (our doing) becomes shaped by who we are (our being).[2] Our being and our doing mutually reinforce one another. The more we practice virtuous habits, the more virtuous we become.

As humans, we both possess virtue as a quality of our character and exercise it through certain practices as an expression of moral action. As Christians, we develop Christlike virtues—faith, hope, and love—by adopting Christlike practices. In this way our minds and hearts become shaped with the instincts and tendencies toward the moral good defined by the life and teaching of Jesus Christ. The ancient Greeks, particularly Aristotle, spoke of people motivated by virtues. Jesus spoke of good people motivated by a good treasury within their hearts. Jesus said to the Pharisees:

You brood of vipers! How can you speak good things, when you are evil? For out of the abundance of the heart the mouth speaks. The good person brings good things out of a good treasure, and the evil person brings evil things out of an evil treasure.

MATTHEW 12:34-35

We speak good things out of the overflow of a good heart, and that good heart is what we mean by virtue. The image of a good heart is not merely a heart scrubbed clean from the stain of sin. A good heart within a good person is a picture of a person who is fully human, a person who is in the process of becoming who God has made that person to be.

Jesus draws a particular interest to the human heart in the Sermon on the Mount when he reframes the law in terms of the disposition of our hearts. Jesus taught us that moral issues are not only things like murder, adultery, and breaking vows but also unvirtuous attributes like anger, lust, and a lack of integrity. Such teaching belongs to the new-covenant work of God. Jeremiah prophesied, "This is the covenant that I will make with the house of Israel after those days, says the LORD: I will put my law within them, and I will write it on their hearts; and I will be their God, and they shall be my people" (Jeremiah 31:33).

According to Jesus, when we carry on with the appearance of moral goodness without the supporting character of heart, we are hypocrites, actors on a stage. Jesus confronted the hypocrisy of the Pharisees with these words:

Woe to you, scribes and Pharisees, hypocrites! For you are like whitewashed tombs, which on the outside look beautiful, but inside they are full of the bones of the dead and of all kinds of filth. So you also on the outside look

righteous to others, but inside you are full of hypocrisy and
lawlessness.

MATTHEW 23:27-28

People who are full of the bones of the dead are not fully alive.
They haven't reached their full capacity as creatures made in the image
of God. They are not virtuous.

Aquinas described two kinds of virtues—moral and theological.
And the moral virtues spring from the theological virtues. Moral
virtues are also called "cardinal virtues." The word *cardinal* comes
from the Latin *cardo*, meaning "hinge." Aquinas's four cardinal virtues include: prudence (wisdom), temperance (self-control), fortitude
(courage), and justice. These four virtues form the hinge on which
all Christian morality swings. These four virtues grow up and flower
from the soil of the three theological virtues: faith, hope, and love.
We call these virtues "theological" because they are God's gifts to us.
We have the responsibility to practice faith, hope, and love but we do
not generate them; we receive them as a gift of grace. The theological
virtues are essential in our connection to God and are the foundation
by which we develop the moral virtues.

Virtue grows by the habits we keep putting down like roots within
our hearts, the core of our being. For followers of the Lamb, virtue is
the condition of our hearts. Biblical writers throughout Scripture use
heart language, which provides us the framework required to reflect
on the Christian virtues of faith, hope, and love. Throughout the
Bible we see the image of the human heart, which is distinct from our
intellect. Possessing moral knowledge isn't the same thing as becoming
a moral person. We can learn about virtue to some degree but becoming a virtuous person is something different. Seeing these references
to the heart helps us grow in our imagination for virtue because we
see that our faith journey is not only an intellectual experience. When

biblical writers describe the heart, they are describing the home of moral virtue within the human soul. Here are a few examples of heart language in the Bible (emphasis added):

- Moses asked, "So now, O Israel, what does the LORD your God require of you? Only to fear the LORD your God, to walk in all his ways, to love him, to serve the LORD your God with all your *heart* and with all your soul" (Deuteronomy 10:12).

- Israel's idolatry, which led to their exile, was rooted in their hearts: "The LORD says: Because they have forsaken my law that I set before them, and have not obeyed my voice, or walked in accordance with it, but have stubbornly followed their own *hearts* and have gone after the Baals, as their ancestors taught them" (Jeremiah 9:13-14).

- In David's prayer of contrition and repentance, he said, "Create in me a clean *heart*, O God, and renew a right spirit within me" (Psalm 51:10, ESV).

- The wisdom of Proverbs guides the wise to "Guard your *heart* above all else, for it determines the course of your life" (Proverbs 4:23, NLT).

- The greatest command, according to Jesus, is to love God "with all your *heart* and with all your soul and with all your mind and with all your strength" (Mark 12:30, ESV).

- As noted above, Jesus referred to virtue as "good treasure" when he described the source of good moral action: "The good person out of the good treasure of his *heart* produces good, and the evil person out of his evil treasure produces evil, for out of the abundance of the *heart* his mouth speaks" (Luke 6:45, ESV).

We want to look at the theological virtues of faith, hope, and love, the first of which is faith. To understand the virtue of faith we have been given, let's take a 360-degree view of it, focusing on four aspects of the faith we have received. We will explore faith as belief, faith as confidence, faith as trust, and faith as allegiance.

FAITH AS BELIEF IN JESUS

Faith is inherently human. While modern skeptics have tried to separate faith from reason, the truth is we all have faith. We all believe in something. We believe that people will follow traffic laws so that we can drive to our destination safely. When we order food at a restaurant, we trust that the kitchen staff will observe proper hygiene. We believe what the preacher says on Sunday morning about the nature of God, and we believe what the doctor says on Tuesday afternoon when the results of our tests are in. We have been given the ability to exercise faith like we have been given the ability to breathe. We believe subconsciously, and when we desire to, we can examine and expand our faith. God has woven faith into the fabric of our very being.

Faith resides in our hearts as a virtue in a way that affects how we think. A belief is an intellectual agreement to the truthfulness of a certain statement. For example, don't judge me, but I believe that pineapple belongs on pizza. In fact, I'd go so far as to make the claim that pineapple is an essential ingredient to really good pizza. If you say to yourself, *I believe that*, then you are expressing intellectual agreement to the truthfulness of that statement. Faith is more than a belief, but it is not less than that.

Faith as a belief is one of many factors that guide the decisions we make.[3] If you don't believe pineapple is essential for good pizza, then you probably won't order it. Our beliefs often work in the background, shaping not only the kind of pizza we order but, more importantly, how we treat people. How you treat people of a different race depends on what you believe about people of a different race. How you treat gay people depends on what you believe about gay people. How you treat people who vote differently than you depends on what you believe about people and their politics.

Every day we face the temptation to put our faith in something—our money, our talents, our ability to be in control, our point of view, our preferred politicians, or the experts within our tribe. While everyone believes something, Christians uniquely believe in Jesus, the Lamb of God, as Lord and Savior. Jesus said, "Do not let your hearts be troubled. Believe in God, believe also in me" (John 14:1). The work of God, according to Jesus, is that we believe (John 6:29). The effort within this task is to keep our belief in Jesus as the Lamb of God central and allow all our other beliefs to fall into orbit around him. I believe Jesus died for our sins in accordance with the Scriptures. I believe he was buried and that he literally, physically, and historically rose from the dead on the third day. If you say you believe those statements, then you are expressing your own intellectual agreement to the truthfulness of what is essential to living life with Jesus at the center.

To believe in Jesus isn't a leap into an unknown abyss. By nature faith—and Christian faith in particular—isn't an impulsive emotional reaction that is opposed to evidence. Perhaps some people in the name of "faith in Jesus" ignore the evidence that has been compiled over two thousand years of Christian history. Or perhaps some people are not aware that the evidence for our faith is rooted in the church's great tradition with its Scriptures, creeds, confessions, councils, prayers, and writings. Furthermore, we have experiential encounters with the living Jesus through worship, the sacraments, and prayer. Jesus isn't merely a person from history we can read about. We worship Jesus as the living Lamb of God, whom we can experience. I believe in Jesus because I sit with him silently in prayer. I believe in Jesus because I commune with him at the celebration of the Lord's Supper. Yet even on days when I don't sense the nearness and closeness of God, I lean on the historical witness of the church testifying to the truthfulness of Jesus. Throughout the centuries, virtuous men and woman have testified to this faith we have received.

FAITH AS CONFIDENCE IN JESUS

I believe Jesus will remain faithful to who he is. As a community of people formed by the Spirit and united by our common faith in Jesus, we believe Jesus will continue to do what he has been doing. Our confidence in Jesus may be mixed with some doubt, which we should expect in our skeptical and critical age. Never in the history of the world has so much information (and disinformation) been available so quickly to so many people. A quick Google search will reveal a counterargument to just about everything. Yet a mixture of faith and doubt has been part of the Jesus movement from the beginning. We have always been a people of belief and doubt.

After Jesus' resurrection, the disciples worshiped him as the slain Lamb of God who had been vindicated in his resurrection, yet some of the disciples experienced doubt.[4] Moving forward, the church Jesus is building would be made up of people who within themselves would experience both faith and doubt. Doubt is not the enemy of faith because each doubt is rooted in confidence in something else. In fact, every doubt is based on an alternative belief.[5] For example, if someone says, "I doubt the resurrection of Jesus because I have never seen someone rise from the dead," they are not rejecting faith per se. Rather this expression of doubt reveals that this person has confidence in what they have personally observed. In other words, this person places confidence in what can be seen. The simple response is to ask, "Do you believe George Washington existed, even though you have not seen him?" To which the skeptic may respond with confidence in American history. A skeptic's doubt reveals faith in something else.

Faith as confidence in Jesus is not opposed to asking questions based on certain doubts we have about God and his activity in the world. Ignoring our doubts is a surefire way to remain in perpetual preadolescence for our entire Christian journey. It's acceptable to reason like a child while we are children, but God wants us to grow up and become mature (1 Corinthians 13:11). Wrestling with doubt is how we grow in faith, but we cannot wrestle forever. Jacob wrestled with God only until the break of day. At some point our wrestling with doubt on a particular issue must end; if not, we become "like a wave of the sea that is driven and tossed by the wind" (James 1:6, ESV). But we can expect to continue to wrestle with God throughout our lifetime over various issues when our experience does not match what we believe about God.

This kind of confidence is a state of being, a true virtue. Faith as confidence in the Lamb of God is a relational quality of our hearts based on past evidence, which enables us to hope in God for the future. We have experienced the presence of Jesus with us in the past, so we are assured he will continue to be with us. The writer of Hebrews defines *faith* as "the assurance of things hoped for, the conviction of things not seen" (Hebrews 11:1). The Greek word translated as "assurance" means substance or foundation.[6] It's a word picture. Think of a substructure of an interstate bridge. Imagine the enormous cement pillars, and corresponding cement footings submerged in the earth, that hold up an overpass used by four lanes of traffic. We don't see the pillars and footings when we are driving over a bridge; they remain unseen. God has driven faith as confidence into the soil of our hearts so that we can become the kind of people who remain faithful to the Lamb, even as we wrestle with doubt. This image is a picture of faith as a virtue.

This kind of faith rejects certitude and the exhausting exercising of trying to feel absolutely sure about our faith in God. Simplistic assurance and endless attempts at feeling secure only lead to emotional burnout and spiritual bankruptcy. Pastor and theologian Greg Boyd admits, "Psychological certainty is inconsequential to the covenantal understanding of faith. The only thing that matters is that a person is *confident enough* of their beliefs *to act* on them."[7] We do not have to understand fully how our beliefs in God mesh with our experience of God in the world. What matters most is "faith expressing itself in love" (Galatians 5:6, NLT). Faith acknowledges doubt and firmly wrestles with it, so that followers of Jesus develop enough confidence in him to act and live a life devoted to centering Jesus.

FAITH AS TRUST IN JESUS

The confidence we have in Jesus cultivates a particular kind of trust in him. Confidence germinates like a seed within us, producing trust, which is known by the way we live. Trust is confidence in motion. We live in a way that only makes sense if the Holy Spirit (who is the Spirit of Jesus) has been poured out on us. Faith as trust in Jesus (based on what we believe about him) is having the confidence to act. Without corresponding action, faith as belief alone is, to quote James, "dead."[8] For example, I could tell you that I believe in the chairs around my dining-room table. I could tell you where we bought them. I could describe in lavish detail the kind of wood they are made from, how they were assembled, and the day we purchased them. But nothing about my belief in the construction of my dining-room chairs proves my confidence in them until I sit on one.

Pursuit of Jesus with this actually-sitting-on-the-chair kind of trust doesn't ensure moral perfection. We fail at times, and people see it. Our beliefs don't always correlate with our actions, and people notice. At times it may feel like our trust in Jesus has been severed by deep disappointment in God. Hiding this disappointment does nothing to help our faith grow. Jesus experienced the feeling of God-forsakenness on the cross when he uttered the words from Psalm 22, "My God, my God, why have you forsaken me?" (Matthew 27:46; Mark 15:34).

If Jesus experienced this profound moment of disillusionment, why should we expect anything different? When we feel disappointed and betrayed, we can at times look to put our trust in imitation saviors, idols that lack the lasting power to save us. Thankfully—and truthfully—God the Father was always present with Jesus, and God is always with us (Psalm 46:1; Matthew 28:20; John 14:18; Hebrews 13:5). God is always near us and always for us. Much like wrestling with doubt, wrestling with disappointment in God gives us the opportunity to heal. As we do, our trust grows, so our fidelity to Jesus is displayed. A watching world can also see a different way to live and love, a way shaped around the life and teaching of Jesus, the Lamb of God.

We see faith as trust when we look at the disciples, who left everything to follow Jesus:

> While walking by the Sea of Galilee, he saw two brothers, Simon (who is called Peter) and Andrew his brother, casting a net into the sea, for they were fishermen. And he said to them, "Follow me, and I will make you fishers of men." Immediately they left their nets and followed him. And going on from there he saw two other brothers, James the son of Zebedee and John his brother, in the boat with Zebedee their father, mending their nets, and he called them. Immediately they left the boat and their father and followed him.
> MATTHEW 4:18-22, ESV

The command to "follow me" evokes trust, confidence, and belief. Why would fishermen leave their fishing business to follow a man they did not trust? Why would they trust a man in whom they had no confidence? Why would they have confidence in someone they did not believe in? From where did this faith come? Matthew offers no description behind the motivation of Peter and Andrew or James and John, but it's safe to assume faith had been born in their hearts. Jesus still extends this invitation. He is still calling us to follow him and walk in his ways.

FAITH AS ALLEGIANCE TO JESUS

Before Jesus called Peter and Andrew, he proclaimed the gospel of the Kingdom: "From that time Jesus began to preach, saying, 'Repent, for the kingdom of heaven is at hand'" (Matthew 4:17, ESV). Our belief, confidence, and trust in Jesus all funnel into allegiance to him. The gospel is the announcement that through his life, death, resurrection, and ascension, Jesus has become King—the King of Israel and the King of the world. Professor Matthew Bates explains: "The gospel reaches its zenith with Jesus' installation and sovereign rule as the Christ, the king. As such, *faith* in Jesus is best described as *allegiance* to him as king."[9] Our response to the gospel is faith—not only as belief, confidence, and trust but as allegiance.

We do trust in Jesus as a loving response to the gospel announcement, but our trust is not merely that Jesus will forgive us of our sins and take us to heaven upon death. Our trust in Jesus is a trust that his Kingdom has come, sins have been forgiven, the life of the age to come is now available, death has been undone, the ruler of this world has been cast out, and we are invited to live in the light of God's Kingdom come to earth. Through our loyalty to the King and his Kingdom, God works to rescue and remake the entire world. Faith is how we pledge allegiance to the Lamb and calibrate our moral lives to the values of God's Kingdom.

Paul sets forth this understanding of faith in the opening of his letter to the Romans:

> Paul, a servant of Christ Jesus, called to be an apostle, set apart for the gospel of God, which he promised beforehand

through his prophets in the holy Scriptures, concerning his
Son, who was descended from David according to the flesh
and was declared to be the Son of God in power according
to the Spirit of holiness by his resurrection from the dead,
Jesus Christ our Lord, through whom we have received
grace and apostleship to bring about the *obedience of faith*
for the sake of his name among all the nations.
ROMANS 1:1-5, ESV, EMPHASIS ADDED

God called Paul to proclaim the gospel in order to produce "obedience of faith," not obedience of belief, confidence, or trust but of
allegiance. Bates adds, "The purpose of the gospel proclamation is to
cultivate obedient allegiance to Jesus the king among the nations."[10]
Unquestionably Jesus wants us to live out what he has taught. Jesus
commissioned us to go into all the world making disciples, "teaching
them to observe all that I have commanded you" (Matthew 28:20,
ESV). But before our obedience he wants our love. "If you love me,"
Jesus said, "you will keep my commandments" (John 14:15).

Allegiance is what we do with our hearts, our passions, our loves,
and our desires. We will never learn the ways of the Lamb until our
allegiance is pledged to him because when we are hard-pressed, we do
what we want to do. What we believe informs our moral decision making, but implementation of that decision comes from our loves and
desires, which have been shaped by our allegiances. As King of kings
and Lord of lords, Jesus will entertain no rival. Splitting our allegiance
between the Kingdom of Heaven and earthly kingdoms weakens our
faith when the storms of stress and the pressure of anxiety settle in.
Hearts formed in the virtue of allegiance to King Jesus alone withstand
the tempests that can disrupt the peace we experience in Jesus.

Faith is integral to what it means to be human. The shape of
Christian faith as a virtue given to us by God can be traced with four
distinct sides—faith as belief, confidence, trust, and allegiance. The

first side is faith as belief, as a conviction regarding the truthfulness of Jesus. As we are convinced that Jesus is who he says he is, we experience faith as confidence in Jesus. We will have questions. As we press on toward Christian maturity we will have doubts, but doubts and questions do not have to shatter our confidence in Jesus' ability to be faithful and present. This confidence provides what we need to trust in King Jesus enough to orient our lives around him. Finally, our faith is a kind of allegiance to King Jesus. We pledge our loyalty to him because we have received this virtue as a gift.

DISCUSSION QUESTIONS

1. Why is moral character important in the Christian life?

2. If faith is inherently human, what are some things people believe that they would not classify as "religious beliefs"?

3. How does wrestling with doubt help us grow in faith?

4. In what ways does our confidence in God serve as pillars that hold us up?

5. Why does it seem empty to claim to trust God but not act on that trust?

6. Have you experienced disappointment with God? Did this experience affect your trust in God?

7. When you consider the word *allegiance*, what is the first thing that comes to mind? How does our understanding of allegiance give shape to our faith?

8. What can you do to grow in the gift of faith?

HOPE IN THE AGE TO COME

Merciful God, who sent your messengers the prophets to
preach repentance and prepare the way for our salvation:
Give us grace to heed their warnings and forsake our sins,
that we may greet with joy the coming of Jesus Christ our
Redeemer; who lives and reigns with you and the Holy Spirit,
one God, now and for ever. Amen.

A COLLECT, SECOND SUNDAY OF ADVENT,
THE BOOK OF COMMON PRAYER

IN ONE OF the more enjoyable scenes from the 1994 film *The Shawshank Redemption*, Ellis Boyd Redding, known as Red, has just been paroled from Shawshank State Penitentiary. We see him riding in the back of a red Ford pickup. Red, played by Morgan Freeman, was making good on a promise he made to his friend Andy Dufresne, played by Tim Robbins. While they were both incarcerated in Shawshank Prison, Andy had asked Red for a favor. He directed Red to find a black rock under a large oak tree at the north end of a long rock wall in a hayfield in Buxton, Maine. He asked Red to go find that rock if he were ever released from prison. Andy assured him that he would find something buried under it.

After exiting the truck, Red walked to the spot Andy had told him about. He found the rock, and under it he found a metal box buried in the dirt. In the box Red discovered a manila envelope filled with cash and a white envelope with a letter from Andy. In the letter, Andy invites Red to break his parole and join him in Mexico. He ends the letter with these words: "Remember, Red, hope is a good thing, maybe the best of things, and no good thing ever dies. I will be hoping that this letter finds you, and finds you well."[1]

I agree with Andy. Hope is indeed a good thing. It's *among* the best things, particularly when things don't seem to be going right. Hope becomes a life preserver that can buoy us above troublesome waters. Hope gives us strength today to continue to press on, even with a mind full of doubt and a heart full of anxiety. Hope is a good thing.

CHRISTIAN HOPE AND FAITH

The hope God gives dwells within followers of Jesus as a virtue. It's a hope based not on what we currently have and can hold in our hands. It's a hope for which we wait. (And I hate waiting.)

This requirement to wait is what makes hope so difficult. It is true that "hope deferred makes the heart sick" (Proverbs 13:12). Deferment, the time between longing for something and its arrival, implies waiting. I have grown in patience, or perhaps I have grown more comfortable with waiting. But I still don't like it, even though I acknowledge the necessity of it.

Much like the capacity to believe, hope is an essential human quality. Without hope we shrivel and shrink into something less than human. In the absence of hope, we slowly settle for the claustrophobic status quo, forgetting that our better selves and a better world await us. Everyone needs hope, but we tend to forget that need until we are facing an unpleasant situation. At least that has been my experience.

When it's a cloudless sunny day and everything seems to be going my way, I can easily convince myself that I don't need hope. It's on a day when the dark clouds roll in and I feel like my entire world is crumbling that I recognize my need for hope. Perhaps you can relate.

Fortunately for us, the hope Jesus offers in his Kingdom announcements in the Sermon on the Mount is not for the rich, the happy, and the boastful. Rather Jesus announces blessings for the poor, the mournful, the meek, those who hunger and thirst for justice, the merciful, the pure in heart, the peacemakers, and the persecuted.

Hope comes alive when we identify with the mournful and the meek even when our lives feel untroubled. When we begin to empathize with people suffering injustice and when our hearts begin to ache for the world to be healed, that's when hope begins to swell.

In the climax of Paul's masterful letter to the Romans, he imagines creation itself waiting and longing for renewal, for freedom from the shackles of decay and destruction. The earth groans for redemption, and we groan for an embodied human experience free from corruption. Paul writes, "In hope we were saved. Now hope that is seen is not hope. For who hopes for what is seen? But if we hope for what we do not see, we wait for it with patience" (Romans 8:24-25).

This God-given hope is more than mere optimism, the general feeling that things will get better. I value optimism in the form of a positive mental attitude, but optimism isn't the same thing as hope from a Christian perspective. Christian hope is an embodied confidence that God will make all things new. What distinguishes Christian hope from feel-good optimism is that Christian hope has its agency and pathways in Jesus. The agency intrinsic in hope is all about power; that is, we have the motivation and ability to go where we need to go to reach a desired future. Pathways are about plans; that is, we know how to reach a desired future. Christian hope recognizes that Jesus has become both the agency within us and the pathway before us to reach God's goal, which is new creation. According to pastor Glenn Packiam, Christian hope is confidence that God will bring about the life of the world to come "by means of what has already been accomplished at the resurrection of Jesus."[2] The power and plans within our hope are rooted in the Spirit who raised Jesus from the dead. The

Spirit nurtures hope deep within our hearts, directing our attention to God's future for us and God's new world.

Christian hope as a virtue is woven within our faith in God. We believe the triune God has both the agency and pathway, the power and plans, to make everything better, to set right everything wrong, and to make all things new. For followers of the Lamb, faith and hope are bound together but oriented differently in relation to time. Faith is a present reality oriented toward the past, what God has done. Hope is a present reality oriented toward the future, what God will do. We put our trust in God and pledge our allegiance to the Lamb based on what God has done in and through Jesus. By his death, resurrection, and ascension, Jesus reigns as King of kings and Lord of lords. These events occurred in history according to the Scriptures and they demonstrate God's enduring faithfulness, so in God we trust. Hope springs up from the ground of faith. We trust God because of what God has done, and we look to the future expecting God to do what he says he will do.

For our family, the biggest test of waiting in hope came with the birth of our middle son, Taylor. When he was two years old, we discovered that he was on the autism spectrum. At age two, he didn't speak and wouldn't even gesture with his hands when he wanted something. When he found himself overwhelmed with anxiety, he would often scream and cry. After speech therapy at our home for a year, Taylor began to point and gesture to communicate things he wanted. He was almost completely nonverbal until he was four. Raising an autistic child was a struggle. We wrestled with what to do. We couldn't shake off the unsettling feeling about his uncertain future. *Would he be able to attend school? Would he be accepted by his peers? Would he be able to graduate from high school? Would he be able to get a job, live on his own, get married?* All these questions raced through our minds.

Taylor was able to attend a mainstream kindergarten class when he was five. He continued to struggle. My wife and I shared in that struggle. Taylor experienced full-scale meltdowns at school and in other public places. We received more than enough unsolicited advice from good-hearted people who knew nothing about autism.

Looking back at those early days of raising an autistic child, I can honestly admit that hope wasn't always strong. My wife and I didn't have the agency or pathway, the power or plans, between the two of us to help our son. We felt despondent and helpless. We had very few options except to trust in God and the teachers, therapists, and other health professionals God sent our way. While in public school, Taylor had an IEP, an Individualized Education Program. During one of our first IEP meetings, we received great advice. One of our IEP team members told us, "You need to have a long-term perspective on Taylor's academic development. There will be lots of bumps along the way. Keep your eyes on the long-term goal of high school graduation." We experienced bumps along the way, no doubt. Taylor progressed through elementary and middle school with lots of meltdowns, set-backs, suspensions, tears, and days of hopelessness.

When Taylor was in eighth grade, I received a call from the school about once a week. On one occasion Taylor had refused a simple task and in anger he kicked over a trash can. Corey Gilpin, his structured learning teacher, asked him to pick up the trash and the can, but Taylor refused. Mr. Gilpin told Taylor that he could not go to his next class until he picked up the trash. Instead of complying, Taylor laid on the floor next to the spilled trash and can, in protest. This wasn't his first time playing possum. I drove down to the school, checked in at the office, and walked to the classroom. All other students had left, and to my surprise, I saw Mr. Gilpin sitting patiently on the floor next to Taylor. I appreciated dedicated teachers like Mr. Gilpin. I then saw Taylor's face and was nearly moved to tears. There was a strange mix-ture of exhaustion, anger, and bewilderment. Taylor didn't know what to do; neither did I. Eventually I was able to coax Taylor to sit up and pick up the trash and the can he kicked over, then we headed home. That was a bad day. We experienced many bad days. Our family shed a lot of tears. We prayed continually. There was nothing else to do but wait, hope in God, and hope that Taylor would begin to mature. Hope kept our attention looking forward—and kept us trusting that God would make all things right eventually.

Four years later, our family sat together in the large civic arena, watching Taylor cross the stage to receive his diploma. I remember the joy I felt in my heart when I heard them read his name. If God provided the power, then people like Corey Gilpin were part of the pathway that gave us hope. Mr. Gilpin wasn't the only part of Taylor's pathway. Caring and dedicated teachers, administrators, paraprofessionals, and therapists were also part of the pathway for our hope. The job for my wife and me during all this time was to wait.

NEW CREATION

Just like I needed a long-term perspective for Taylor's development, we as Christians need a long-term vision for our lives with God. *What does our future look like as followers of the Lamb? What will God do in the future?* Some of the future is still veiled, but one thing we know is that God will make all things new. This expectation was in Isaiah's vision, when he heard the Lord explain, "I am about to create new heavens and a new earth; the former things shall not be remembered or come to mind" (Isaiah 65:17). In this new creation, we find our purpose, living full human lives:

> No more shall there be in it an infant that lives but a few days, or an old person who does not live out a lifetime; for one who dies at a hundred years will be considered a youth, and one who falls short of a hundred will be considered accursed. They shall build houses and inhabit them; they shall plant vineyards and eat their fruit.
> ISAIAH 65:20-21

We will find true peace in this world of new creation because on that day "the wolf and the lamb shall feed together, the lion shall eat straw like the ox; but the serpent—its food shall be dust! They shall not hurt or destroy on all my holy mountain, says the LORD" (Isaiah 65:25). We wait in hope for that day, and we embody that hope now as we wait.

We look forward with eager hearts for the re-creation of heaven and earth, so our hope is an embodied hope, the hope of a newly made earth where God dwells with his people, as John the Revelator saw in his heavenly vision:

> Then I saw a new heaven and a new earth; for the first heaven and the first earth had passed away, and the sea was no more. And I saw the holy city, the new Jerusalem, coming down out of heaven from God, prepared as a bride adorned for her husband. And I heard a loud voice from the throne saying,
>
> > "See, the home of God is among mortals.
> > He will dwell with them as their God;
> > they will be his peoples,
> > and God himself will be with them;
> > he will wipe every tear from their eyes.
> > Death will be no more;
> > mourning and crying and pain will be no more,
> > for the first things have passed away."
>
> And the one who was seated on the throne said, "See, I am making all things new." Also he said, "Write this, for these words are trustworthy and true."
> REVELATION 21:1-5

While we wait for the full expression of God's new creation, God allows us to experience the firstfruits of new creation now. Paul writes, "So if anyone is in Christ, there is a new creation: everything old has passed away; see, everything has become new" (2 Corinthians 5:17). Waiting becomes more tolerable as we begin to see the signs of new creation within our own lives. We don't see the totality of new creation, but as we increasingly grow into the likeness of Jesus, we do get to see the first glimpses of Isaiah's vision of people no longer hurting or destroying one another. We get to see our purpose as flourishing human beings created in the image of pure love.

As we embody the ways of Jesus now, we get to see the kind of peace where the wolf and lamb eat together and where humans don't harm or destroy one another. If we keep our eyes on God's future work of new creation, that vision shapes how we live today. We are the new-creation people who don't harm or destroy but instead create communities of kindness. We patiently wait as hope is renewed within us, and we follow the Lamb of God that we might be found as people who live at peace. According to Peter, "We wait for new heavens and a new earth, where righteousness is at home. Therefore, beloved, while you are waiting for these things, strive to be found by him at peace, without spot or blemish" (2 Peter 3:13-14). We wait in hope as a peaceable people formed by a peaceable Kingdom. We live as ambassadors of peace now because if God's new creation is a song, then the peace is the melody.

FROM HEAVEN TO EARTH

For years I have heard countless Christians talk about the hope of heaven, the hope of escaping this corrupt world and going to our "heavenly home." Certainly the promise of Jesus' presence upon death is a great comfort that we never want to set aside. While good and true, the hope of heaven isn't our ultimate or even our primary hope as we look to the future. In the words of N. T. Wright, "Heaven is important but it's not the end of the world."[3] The world of space, matter, and time will not suddenly end and then we live forever with God in a faraway place called "heaven." Christians have historically centered their hope on the Lamb of God, Jesus, who is our blessed hope:

> The grace of God has appeared, bringing salvation for all people, training us to renounce ungodliness and worldly passions, and to live self-controlled, upright, and godly lives in the present age, waiting for our blessed hope, the appearing of the glory of our great God and Savior Jesus Christ.
>
> TITUS 2:11-13, ESV

Jesus will appear at some point in the future. The Greek noun translated "appearing" was used in the first-century Greek world to describe "the glorious manifestation of the gods."[4] It is used in the New Testament exclusively to describe the future unveiling of Jesus in his glory as King of kings and Lord of lords. We believe Jesus is Lord now. We believe Jesus currently reigns as King of the world, but it is as if a large, thick, dark cosmic curtain has obscured our view. In a moment, in a twinkling of the eye, the curtain will be lifted and Jesus will appear. Until that time, we wait.

Jesus rules from heaven, but heaven and earth are not galaxies apart. Heaven isn't really that far away; it's just on the other side of the curtain. Like C. S. Lewis's magical world of Narnia, heaven is just through the backside of the wardrobe. Right now Jesus is out of sight, but the grace of God has appeared, and it's training us to reject everything that does not reflect God's image: ungodly, evil desires like obsession with money, sex, power, greed, pleasure, and/or dominance. The appearance of God's grace is also training us to live godly lives now, while we wait in hope.

The blessed hope is not that we are going to heaven but that Jesus is coming to earth. From the fourth century onward, Christians have confessed, "[Jesus] will come again in glory to judge the living and the dead, and his kingdom will have no end."[5] Matthew rightly calls Jesus' Kingdom the "kingdom of heaven" (Matthew 3:2). Note, however, that it's not a kingdom *in* heaven but a kingdom *from* heaven. The trajectory of our hope is not God whisking us away to heaven, but the King of heaven coming to earth, which is why day-by-day we pray, *Your kingdom come. Your will be done,* on earth *as in heaven.* The popular idea of a secret return of Jesus and a literal snatching away of Christians while unsuspecting sinners are left behind is rooted neither in Scripture nor in church history. Our hope is not that we are going but that Jesus is coming—because he himself is our hope.

LIVING AT THE OVERLAP OF AGES

We believe the blessed hope of Jesus' appearing will fully usher in the age to come. The word we use to describe our view of the last things is *eschatology.* First-century Jewish eschatology was built around the concepts of "this age" and "the age to come," that is, the present evil age and the age to come, where the Messiah, the Jewish King, reigns. This age and the age to come is how Jesus and all the New Testament writers understood present and future time.[6]

Modern American evangelicals have been so preoccupied with heaven and hell and who goes where in the end that they have missed the paradigm used by Jesus and the apostles—the present age and the age to come. For example, Jesus promised, "I am with you always, to the end of the age" (Matthew 28:20). In one sense the age to come had broken into the present evil age because Jesus the Messiah *had come.* In another sense the age to come is still a future event because Jesus will come again. Both realities are true, so we find ourselves living with one foot planted in this age and the other firmly planted in the age to come. We derive our identity from that future world, rejecting this present evil age and its corrupting influence.

If we have been united with Christ Jesus through baptism and we have been seated with Jesus where he is reigning and ruling, then we have been ushered into the age to come. Yet we still live in this present evil age. We have a strange dual citizenship: We belong to the future where Jesus reigns and, at the same time, we have homes in this broken-down world. In this way, we live at the overlap of the ages, embodying the values of the age to come and living them out in this present age. In the words of Paul to Titus, we "live lives that are self-controlled, upright, and godly" because we live in the light of God's new world (Titus 2:12).

Ethics follows eschatology. Hope in God's new creation is a present reality for us, so it shapes how we live today. Our ethical values do not come from this present evil age, but from the age to come. For example, we live as a nonantagonistic, nonretaliatory, nonviolent, peaceable people because according to Isaiah's vision, in the age to come, we won't hurt or destroy any more in God's holy mountain.[7]

We follow the teachings of Jesus and promote peace in this present evil age because we belong to the age to come. We live at the overlap of these two ages, so we do make some concessions. We live as a peaceable people, but we still have police officers who carry guns. The ruling authorities don't bear the sword in vain. All swords will eventually be beaten into plowshares, but until then we concede to use them sparingly. Followers of Jesus serve as the moral compass of this world, by calibrating our moral orientation according to the values of the Kingdom. If God has placed the sword in the hands of the state, then we who are followers of Jesus are the voice of Jesus to Peter saying, "put away the sword" (Matthew 26:52, author's paraphrase). We can be a voice of moral constraint in a violent world if we allow our ethical values to flow from the age to come. We live as peacemakers in this present age because we put our hope in the coming of Jesus, the Lamb of God who was slain. We start with what life is like in the age to come and then we make small incremental concessions in this present age, acknowledging that we will not all agree on what those concessions look like. The hope that God gives can unite us through our disagreements. This hope nestled in our hearts empowers us to keep our eyes focused on the future, where a better day is coming.

God gives us this hope as a virtue. Our response to this gift is to find the joy in waiting. Much like my wife and I had to wait as we watched our autistic son struggle through school, followers of the Lamb have to wait for the world to become new. We do have the opportunity to participate in God's work of new creation because we belong to the age to come. But our participation doesn't negate the waiting. The joy that I have found in waiting in hope is the joy of God's presence. As I have cultivated habits of prayer and awareness that open me up more fully to the presence of God, I have experienced an abiding joy in knowing God is with me. I have yet to be perfected in patience. I have moments of agitation, but when I slow down and breathe, and lift up my head to acknowledge God's presence, I feel the abiding joy that gives me the patience to wait in hope.

DISCUSSION QUESTIONS

1. What book or film offers images of hope for you?

2. Do you consider yourself a patient person? Describe a time when you patiently waited for something in hope.

3. Why does having hope require both power and plans?

4. How does the vision of new creation cause hope to grow in you today?

5. What are the differences between the popular hope of going to heaven and the more biblical hope of heaven coming to earth?

6. What does it look like for us to live at the overlap of the present evil age and the age to come?

7. What does it look like for us to receive our values from God's new creation, that is, God's future world?

8. What can you do this week to grow in hope?

LOVE IN THE WAY
OF THE LAMB

O Lord, you have taught us that without love whatever we
do is worth nothing: Send your Holy Spirit and pour into
our hearts your greatest gift, which is love, the true bond
of peace and of all virtue, without which whoever lives is
accounted dead before you. Grant this for the sake of your
only Son Jesus Christ, who lives and reigns with you and the
Holy Spirit, one God, now and for ever. Amen.

A COLLECT, SEVENTH SUNDAY AFTER THE EPIPHANY,
THE BOOK OF COMMON PRAYER

OVER THE YEARS I have met more than one person who was
traumatized by a false view of God, one that portrays the God and
Father of our Lord Jesus as harsh, critical, and cruel. Some who have
remained in the faith have even commented that while they love Jesus,
they still live with the fear of disappointing Jesus' Father. Bad theology
is an unforgiving slave driver.

My faith journey has been different. My first steps in pursuing
Jesus began as I was plunged into God's love. What drew me to Jesus
was the love and acceptance he offered. As an awkward teenager, I
was searching for a place of belonging. I didn't quite find my place
among the academic elites or the gifted athletes in my high school. I
was smart, but not that smart. I loved sports, but I wasn't that athletic.
I felt like a ship at sea with no port to call home.

Without a sense of belonging, I questioned my value as well as my capacity to experience love. Then I heard the words of the gospel, "For God so loved . . ." (John 3:16). I initially accepted the claims of the Christian faith not because it squelched some nagging intellectual questioning but because I experienced love, the love of God revealed in Jesus and made known by the Holy Spirit. Years later I would wrestle with the big questions of life—God, suffering, meaning, purpose, loss, and disappointment—but what has tethered me to the ancient Christian faith has been my experience of the God who is love.

The love God shares with us is the most foundational of all Christian virtues. As followers of the Lamb, we grow our moral lives out of the soil of love. Remember Aquinas called faith, hope, and love the theological virtues in that they are God's virtues given to us as we participate in the life of God. He described these virtues as the way we can become partakers of God's very nature.[1] We participate in the life of God like a piece of wood participates in a fire. The wood is not by nature fire, but it participates in fire and becomes consumed and ultimately transformed by fire. God is by nature love. As we practice the virtue of love given to us by God, we are being consumed by love's flames. We are transformed by them, not into ash as with the fire but into Christlikeness. We also practice faith and hope, but loving in the way of the Lamb distinctly shapes us into people marked by love. Paul writes, "Now faith, hope, and love abide, these three; but the greatest of these is love" (1 Corinthians 13:13, ESV). Love isn't greater because faith and hope don't matter. Love is greater because, of all the theological virtues, love is who God is in God's very triune nature. When we participate in the love God gives us, we participate in the very life of God.

All God is doing, and all God has done, comes from love, so that no act of God can ever be deemed unloving. Even God's judgment is an expression of his love. We esteem God's acts of judgment, both past and future, not in *contrast to* God's love but in harmony with it. God is not love and also justice and judgment. Rather, God is love who *displays* his love in acts of justice and judgment. God isn't like an unhealthy parent who disciplines his children out of anger. When God disciplines us, we receive it as love, "for the Lord disciplines those whom he loves, and chastises every child whom he accepts" (Hebrews 12:6). Nowhere do we see God's love on clearer display than when we gaze on the Lamb of God on the cross. Paul writes:

> While we were still weak, at the right time Christ died for the ungodly. For one will scarcely die for a righteous person— though perhaps for a good person one would dare even to die—but God shows his love for us in that while we were still sinners, Christ died for us.
> ROMANS 5:6-8, ESV

King Jesus didn't die for us because we were good enough, or because we were righteous, holy, and pure enough. He didn't die for us because of our great love for God and fidelity to walk in all his ways. He didn't die for us because God was obligated to punish someone. Rather Jesus died for us as the sacrificial Lamb when we were drowning in a sea of sin. Jesus died to rescue us and free us from the tightening noose of sin and corruption. Sin was the problem for which the Cross was the solution. Jesus' death on the cross became the definition of what love looks like. The love we have received as a virtue is a sacrificial love. It is a love that suffers for us, a love that suffers *with us*. It is a love that is self-giving. The Holy Spirit invites us into this love, the circle of love demonstrated on the cross and shared between the Father, Son, and Holy Spirit. When we participate in that love, it overtakes us. When we receive this virtue of love, we become a virtuous people who love God, our neighbors, and our enemies.

WHAT'S LOVE GOT TO DO WITH IT?

Paul offers the most colorful and Jesus-centered description of love in 1 Corinthians 13. This passage has become a favorite at weddings, but Paul wrote it to show the Christians in Corinth how to exercise the gifts of the Holy Spirit to build up the church. Paul encourages this local church to think of itself as a body with many different parts, where "the eye cannot say to the hand, 'I have no need of you'" (1 Corinthians 12:21). All the gifts of the Spirit—even prophesying, performing miracles, healing the sick, and speaking in tongues—have their place in the life of the church, but only if Christians practice them in the context of love. Paul writes:

> If I speak with human eloquence and angelic ecstasy but don't love, I'm nothing but the creaking of a rusty gate.
>
> If I speak God's Word with power, revealing all his mysteries and making everything plain as day, and if I have faith that says to a mountain, "Jump," and it jumps, but I don't love, I'm nothing.
>
> If I give everything I own to the poor and even go to the stake to be burned as a martyr, but I don't love, I've gotten nowhere. So, no matter what I say, what I believe, and what I do, I'm bankrupt without love.
>
> 1 CORINTHIANS 13:1-3, MSG

Paul then goes on to describe love[2] in a way that mirrors the words and work of Jesus:

Paul said, "Love never gives up."
Jesus said, "Remain in my love" (John 15:9, NLT).

Paul said, "Love cares more for others than for self."
Jesus said, "No one has greater love than this, to lay down one's life
for one's friends" (John 15:13).

Paul said, "Love doesn't want what it doesn't have."
Jesus said, "One's life does not consist in the abundance of
possessions" (Luke 12:15).

Paul said, "Love doesn't strut, doesn't have a swelled head,
doesn't force itself on others."
Jesus said, "Take my yoke upon you, and learn from me; for I am
gentle and humble in heart" (Matthew 11:29).

Paul said, "Love . . . isn't always 'me first,' doesn't fly off the
handle, doesn't keep score of the sins of others."
Jesus told the woman caught in the act of adultery, "Neither do
I condemn you" (John 8:11).

Paul said, "Love . . . doesn't revel when others grovel, takes
pleasure in the flowering of truth."
Jesus said, "I am the way, the truth, and the life" (John 14:6, NLT).

Paul said, "Love . . . puts up with anything, trusts God always,
always looks for the best."
Jesus prayed in the garden, "Not my will but yours be done"
(Luke 22:42).

Paul said, "Love . . . never looks back, but keeps going to
the end."
Jesus said, "I am with you always, to the end of the age"
(Matthew 28:20).

Paul said, "Love never dies."
Jesus, the embodiment of love, went into the bowels of death,
where death itself could not contain the presence of
pure love.

Our task is to keep love from devolving into mere sentimentality or infatuation. Love certainly is an emotion. We feel love for our favorite sports team. We feel loved by those we are emotionally close to. Healthily married couples experience and demonstrate affectionate and romantic love within their marriage. The feeling of love belongs in God's good creation, but the love we seek to participate in surpasses the love we feel. The love described by Paul in 1 Corinthians is the cruciform love we see displayed by Jesus, the sacrificial Lamb.

The love we have received as a virtue is a choice. We determine whether to walk in the way of love or wither away in apathy. Love in the way of Jesus is a commitment because it persists and endures in the face of hardship. Love is an action because it seeks expression. God, who is love, was content with the love shared between the Father, Son, and Spirit, but that love sought expression in the creation of the world and humanity. Love is a verb, but first it's a virtue. Before we demonstrate our love in acts of kindness, we become people of love who reflect the God who made us. One of the beautiful elements of Christian discipleship is the empowerment we receive to do what Jesus calls us to do. Not only does Jesus command us to love God, our neighbors, and even our enemies but Jesus promises to enable us to have the capacity to love (Romans 5:5). We love God and others with the love God has given us.

Love as a virtue that governs our hearts and shapes our moral decision-making finds a home deep within the core of our being, much deeper than love as an emotion, action, or intention. Dallas Willard describes love as the "overall disposition of the human self."[3] Certainly we have the capacity to grow in love throughout our

Christian journey, but as love becomes the primary characteristic of our hearts, it becomes our natural response to the world around us.

Love as a virtue as described by Paul and other New Testament writers supersedes mere duty or obligation. N. T. Wright explains: "The love of which Paul speaks is clearly a *virtue*. It is not a 'rule' of the sort that is so out of fashion nowadays, imposed in an arbitrary fashion and to be obeyed out of a sense of duty."[4] Rule-based religion squeezes the life and love out of the Christian faith. Love cannot be reduced to a simple moral code detailing what we should and should not do. God planted love in our hearts. As the love of God grows, it blossoms into beautiful actions of mercy and kindness. According to Wright, "Love is a virtue. It is a language to be learned, a musical instrument to be practiced, a mountain to be climbed via some steep and tricky cliff paths but with the most amazing view from the top."[5]

Love as a language, instrument, or mountain hike shapes our character so that we become like native speakers, musical marvels, and seasoned mountaineers who act and do instinctually. The virtue of love is what Methodist founder John Wesley meant by the phrase *Christian perfection* in his classic work *A Plain Account of Christian Perfection*.

Wesley responded to the moral laxity of his generation with a call for what he termed "scriptural holiness," that is, a holiness defined by Scripture.[6] For Wesley, followers of Jesus were called to pursue perfection not according to rigid moral rules but according to love. Wesley defined *perfection* as "loving God with all our heart, mind, soul, and strength" and explains, "This implies that no wrong temper, none contrary to love, remains in the soul; and that all the thoughts, words and actions, are governed by pure love."[7] Wesley understood perfection in terms of maturity, of reaching our full potential. And he described this maturity not as perfection in action but as perfection of the soul in love. For Wesley, Christian perfection was a picture of the entirety of one's life enveloped in the fire of Trinitarian love, where all that marred God's image in us is burned up. When we are filled with the Spirit, our hearts are inflamed with the fire of love.[8]

HABITS OF LOVE

Loving in the way of the Lamb is a virtue we experience by our union with the triune God, but we do not instantly become people of love on the day we are baptized. We can experience God's grace and receive God's forgiveness as a gift from the Holy Spirit. Yet the degree to which the virtue of love takes root and expands is based on the habits we keep. Virtues are neither all doing nor all being. Instead, our being and doing exist in symbiosis. We receive love as a gift—and then, as we practice love, we become more loving. We receive mercy from God, which motives us to be merciful; and the more we engage in merciful acts, the more merciful we become. We can choose to work with God's empowering grace producing love within us, or we can work against it. From Cyprian in the third century to Aquinas in the thirteenth century, ancient Christians saw value in practicing Christian habits because they saw it as the way to participate in the Holy Spirit's work.[9] A linguist becomes an expert in a language by conversing in it as often as possible. A musician masters an instrument by practicing scales and songs on it regularly for years. A mountaineer grows in strength by working out months before conquering a mountain. We become people of love by practicing habits of love.

Marriage has been an opportunity for me to practice the habits of love for nearly thirty years. In an interview with *Plough Quarterly*, theologian Stanley Hauerwas called the idea of falling in love as the prerequisite to marriage a "deep bedevilment." Christian marriage, according to Hauerwas, is rooted in something deeper and richer than infatuation. For Hauerwas, "Marriage is not something to be done because two people think they love one another. Rather it's based on faithfulness to one another in the community such that over a lifetime, we're able to look back on the relationship and call it love."[10] Far from the limitations of sentimentality around marriage frequently displayed in our society, spouses loving each other in the way of Jesus is a picture of faithfulness and service in a Christian marriage.

After twenty-eight years of marriage, I can testify that what I called love nearly three decades ago was nothing more than a passing shadow compared to the lifelong faithfulness I call love today. The depth of love that my wife, Jenni, and I share today has come about by the habits of love we have learned and practiced in our marriage. These habits aren't specific to marriage. We can also practice them with our family, friends, and neighbors. Marriage has become an idol for some who hold it up as the gold standard of Christian maturity. I know many sincere followers of Jesus who are single and who live vibrant lives of love. These habits are for all of us. Here are ten habits of love we can practice to grow in the Jesus-shaped virtue of love.

1. *Saying "I love you" at the end of each conversation.* My wife and I say "I love you" at the end of nearly every conversation, whether we are on the phone or face to face. In fact, if I don't hear those words, then I know something is wrong!

   It's easy for married couples to say "I love you" because there is an established relationship where saying such things is likely the norm. Saying "I love you" is much more difficult with friends we go to church with or work with because we experience different levels of intimacy with our friends. Expressing our love to the people in our lives requires us to know them and the context of our relationship. Once I feel comfortable with the closeness of a friendship and am reasonably confident that my friend feels the same, then I'm quick to say "I love you." We all know love is more than words, but it is not less. Saying it when appropriate is a key habit of love.

2. *Checking in throughout the day.* From the beginning of our marriage Jenni and I have kept short accounts with each other. Texting has made that so much easier these days. It really is rare for the two of us to go more than four or five hours without checking in with each other, either by text, phone call, or in person.

The "check-in" can become a habit of love whenever we reach out to anyone to see how they are doing. A quick text to ask "How are you doing today?" could be the most loving experience a friend of yours has in their busy day. This practice keeps us focused outward, so that we do not drown in thoughts of ourselves.

3. *Sharing words of encouragement.* We live at a time when sarcasm and the art of the insult is entertainment. I understand. I enjoy teasing my friends, and my wife has certainly been the recipient of unwelcomed sarcasm from me. We can laugh as we are teased, until the laughter runs out—and often it does.

When we share words of encouragement, they settle down deep in the hearts of those we love. Even if words of affirmation are not our primary love language,[11] most of us could use words of encouragement from time to time. When people who know us well see something positive in us and point it out, love abounds. The power of this kind of noticing and encouragement should not be underestimated.

4. *Scheduling time to be together.* Jenni and I have developed intimacy and deep-level companionship through the necessary combination of open and honest communication and time spent together. Early in our marriage, we discovered the beauty of the lunch date, scheduling time in the middle of the day to be together. After all these years, I still look forward to our date lunches!

Couples can certainly learn how to express their thoughts and feelings effectively, but if they don't carve out time in their schedule for uninterrupted time to be together, they won't have a moment to communicate. We communicate love for one another when we make plans to do things together. Friendships are built around common interests, and for friendships to grow, someone must take the initiative to plan to engage in that interest together.

5. *Praying every day.* It's common for couples to make praying together a central part of their marriage. I celebrate when couples regularly pray together, but this kind of prayer is not something that Jenni and I have done throughout the years.

   What I have done is develop the habit of praying for my wife—and each of my family members—by name every day. I have a regular time in morning prayer where I pray for the people I love. I pray for my family, for my church, and for people in need. When I pray for my family, I ask God to bless, provide for, and protect each of them. As specific situations arise for a family member, I add a request for that. Praying for my loved ones regularly is one of the ways I demonstrate my love for them.

6. *Doing things without being asked.* When you have spent enough time with someone, you begin to learn their routines and preferences. Jenni and I both enjoy our morning coffee. I'm the first to roll out of bed 99.9 percent of the time, so I prepare the Keurig for her every morning. I fill the machine with freshly filtered water, grind coffee beans, load up her reusable K-Cup, find a sixteen-ounce coffee mug, and place it on the machine so when she wakes up, all she needs to do is hit the start button. Jenni never has to ask me to prep the Keurig. I have grown to anticipate her needs. A thoughtfulness

is communicated in this habit of love. Of course we appreciate it when our friends come through for us when we make a "big ask." But how much more of our love is communicated when we do something for them before they ask?

7. *Seeking to serve first.* Jesus said, "The greatest among you will be your servant" (Matthew 23:11). A great marriage that is rooted in the ways of Jesus looks like two servants trying to outdo the other in serving one another. We serve not to manipulate someone into doing what we want but simply for the benefit of that person.

Love grows through acts of service. Imagine what it would look like if every member of a family, a friend group, or a local church agreed to seek to be the first one to serve. Can you imagine the kind of love that would be experienced in an environment like that? A single act of service in a life otherwise void of service can feel empty. But seeking to serve first over a lifetime feels like a Jesus kind of love.

8. *Listening, just listening.* Healthy communication includes a back and forth process of talking and listening. For a long time into our marriage, I focused my attention on what *I* was saying. I had something to say, and I wanted to be sure Jenni would hear. Sadly this approach only led to arguments and misunderstandings. Since then, I have discovered the kind of love we experience through understanding, not just through being understood. I understand best when I listen well.

Listening is so close to loving that most people cannot tell the difference.[12] Healthy listening requires us to cultivate the difficult art of restraint, setting aside our agenda, our opinions and judgments in order to open ourselves to another person. When we listen to empathize, we allow love to flourish.

9. *Asking loving questions.* Perhaps the most important habit I have developed in seeking understanding and active listening is asking loving questions. Merely asking any sort of question isn't sufficient. I have learned how to ask *loving* questions, because a question like "Why are you so stupid?" isn't helpful. Questions like that one, and even less obvious ones, are accusations hidden within the pretense of a question. Loving questions like "I'm having trouble following; can you explain that again?" lead to more understanding. When my wife and I are in an emotionally charged conversation and I feel confused and anxious or don't know what to say, I look for a loving question to ask. Questions bring us closer together. Words of accusation push us apart, putting a dagger into the heart of love.

10. *Asking for forgiveness.* Conflict is inevitable in any relationship, even healthy ones. Most of us would prefer to avoid it, but conflict itself isn't bad. What is good or bad is how we *respond* to conflict. The habit I have learned over the years is to meet conflict with understanding, empathy, and communication. Once I recognize my fault, I express three phrases—I understand. I am sorry. Will you forgive me? I start by expressing that I understand that my actions, whether they were unintentional or not, have caused harm. Next is the apology: "I am sorry." Apologies are a helpful starting point but they are insufficient for reconciliation because the typical response to someone saying "I am sorry" is "It's okay." In addition to offering an apology, I ask, "Will you forgive me?" This question prompts the person who was hurt or frustrated in the relational conflict to respond. This habit is fundamental because in the words of Nobel Peace Prize recipient Desmond Tutu, "Without forgiveness, without reconciliation, we have no future."[13]

Practicing habits like these will form us into the kind of love Jesus demonstrated. These habits get at the heart of the others-oriented love of the Lamb. Along with faith and hope, love rounds out the three theological virtues, which are the foundation for our ethical decision making. As we grow as faithful, hopeful, and loving people, we develop the moral instincts that empower us to walk in the ways of Jesus, who, as the Lamb of God, demonstrated faithfulness, hope, and love for the sake of the world God loves.

DISCUSSION QUESTIONS

1. Outside of God, your family, and friends, what is one thing you love? How do people know you love it?

2. How does the love we receive from God enable us to participate in the life of God?

3. How do you see God's love expressed in our world and in your life?

4. How does Jesus' death display God's love?

5. What are the key differences between love as an emotion and love as a virtue?

6. Of the ten habits of love described in this chapter, which one is the easiest for you to practice?

7. Which of these habits challenge you the most?

8. Which of these ten habits do you need to focus on first? How can you implement that habit into your life?

OUR COMMON LIFE TOGETHER

WHEN WE ARE out to eat, my wife has a habit of noticing people eating alone. Meals are meant to be shared. We increase the enjoyment that comes from food when we eat in the company of our friends. Her instinctual draw toward people in isolation comes from a deep place. Even if a person chooses to live a solitary lifestyle—eating alone, working alone, living alone—it doesn't seem quite right.

As an introvert, I understand how times of isolation can be strengthening. I love people, but after a long day of nonstop social interactions, I often feel "peopled out." Nevertheless I have long recognized my need for other people. We are, after all, dependent creatures. I need people to help, challenge, encourage, lead, follow, and love me. We were made for each other.

We are our truest selves when we rightly reflect God's image in the way we love. The triune God, who is himself a community of Father, Son, and Holy Spirit, has made us from this pattern. If God is relational in God's very essence and being, then we who bear his image can expect to be relational.

Loving God as an isolated individual and despising humanity is not the way to experience the life Jesus offers. The apostle John advised, "Those who say, 'I love God,' and hate their brothers or sisters, are liars; for those who do not love a brother or sister whom they have seen, cannot love God whom they have not seen" (1 John 4:20). We express our love for God in how we love other people. When we love others well, we are living in harmony with our identity as image bearers of God.

The primary opportunity Christians have to love our brothers and sisters is through the weekly gathering we call church. This united family exists as an alternative society based on faith, hope, and love. God's Kingdom depends on the church being a socially diverse and multiethnic family where people whom the world tries to divide are united around the throne of the Lamb. Currently, the church remains afloat in a sea of uncertainty. She has been beaten and battered by self-inflicted wounds, criticism from those on the outside, and abandonment by those who have walked out of her doors. Yet for all her imperfection, failures, and scars, I still believe in the church. I believe in the endurance and necessity of the church. It's the only community I trust to be a lasting demonstration of true human flourishing, one known by the way we love one another in community. When Jesus taught us to pray, the first word he taught us to say is *our*, not *my*, *me*, *mine*, or *I*. Prayer in the way of Jesus begins with a community of intentional love created by God for his purposes.

Not only do we flourish when we rightly love our brothers and sisters in Christ, but we also support a flourishing society when we live in right relationship with people outside the church. Our common life includes loving our neighbors as ourselves. This is what it looks like to practice justice. We need one another for society to function health-ily. Dr. Martin Luther King Jr. famously wrote, "We are caught in an inescapable network of mutuality, tied in a single garment of destiny. Whatever affects one directly affects all indirectly."[14] This "network of mutuality" is why the God of Israel instructed the exiles in Babylon to pray for the city, to build houses, plant gardens, and have kids. Their flourishing as the people of God was tied to the flourishing of the pagan city where they lived (Jeremiah 29:5-7).

Our identity as followers of the Lamb is rooted in the identity of the ancient people of God. We are called today to love our neighbors by lending a hand—by serving others and helping those in need. To that end, we advocate for justice in the name of Jesus. We acknowl-edge, in the words of Dr. King, that "injustice anywhere is a threat to justice everywhere."[1] We carry out our work for justice in the *name* of Jesus, not by force or coercion but in the gentle *ways* of Jesus. This advocacy also includes our engagement in politics for the sake of the *polis*, the city.

As we consider centering Jesus in our common life together, we will start by locating Jesus at the center of our time spent gathered in worship. We will explore what it looks like to worship in a Jesus-centered church. From there we will look at the biblical concept of justice and imagine what our advocacy for justice looks like when we keep Jesus at the center of it. Finally, we will enter the political arena, where we will compare the divisiveness of modern American politics with the reconciling politics of the Lamb.

A JESUS KIND OF CHURCH

*Almighty and everlasting God, in Christ you have revealed
your glory among the nations: Preserve the works of your
mercy, that your Church throughout the world may persevere
with steadfast faith in the confession of your Name; through
Jesus Christ our Lord, who lives and reigns with you and the
Holy Spirit, one God, for ever and ever. Amen.*

A COLLECT, PROPER 24,
THE BOOK OF COMMON PRAYER

THE CHURCH HAS BEEN my extended family my entire adult
life. I didn't grow up in the church as a child. I was baptized when I
was eleven, and it wasn't until I was a teenager that church became
a regular part of my life. My wife and I met as teenagers in a church
youth group. We have often commented on how much of our lives
is intertwined with the church. I sensed a call to pastoral ministry
when I was sixteen years old, got married in the church when I was
twenty, and was ordained into full-time vocational ministry when I
was twenty-five. I have raised children with the support of the church
and now our adult son and his wife are raising our grandchild in
the church.

The church has loved us and been good to us. The church was
there when my wife and I didn't know what we were doing as young

parents. The church was there through our middle son's journey through a congenital heart defect and autism. The church was there to teach me how to be a pastor when, in my twenties, I was still trying to figure out who I was. Despite all these positive personal experiences, I realize that most of us have been disappointed by the church at some point or other. And yet many of us have also healed and grown in the body of Christ. It's hard to imagine life without the church!

I suppose I still believe in the church because the local church (and by extension, its global expression) lies at the heart of God's new creation project. With the birth of Jesus, the world experienced the dawn of new creation. Jesus did not come into our broken-down world to condemn it; rather, in the words of John, Jesus came "in order that the world might be saved through him" (John 3:17). Jesus' saving work plants seeds of new life, seeds of redemption, that will sprout and grow into God's purposes for all creation to be renewed. The church has been God's primary gardening tool toward that end. The seduction of secularism continues to lure people into a churchless spirituality, yet Jesus continues to do what he has always been doing—building the church. As Simon Peter declared, "[He is] the Messiah, the Son of the living God" (Matthew 16:16). Jesus immediately blessed Peter after this confession of faith:

> Blessed are you, Simon son of Jonah! For flesh and blood has not revealed this to you, but my Father in heaven. And I tell you, you are Peter, and on this rock I will build my church, and the gates of Hades will not prevail against it.
> MATTHEW 16:17-18

The confession that Jesus is the Jewish Messiah and the world's true King becomes the foundation on which Jesus builds his church. Through it, he pushes God's new creation project forward. Jesus has been, and Jesus is still, building his church.

As followers of Jesus we have great freedom to imagine and reimagine what church like looks like within our particular cultural context, but the church Jesus is building is at its core an embodied gathering of the baptized people of God where, in the words of Protestant reformer John Calvin, God's Word is rightly preached and heard, and the sacraments are administered.[1] Churches within North America may look different from one another. They certainly look different from many churches elsewhere in the world. On any given Sunday morning, God's people could gather to worship in a beautiful historic building or a renovated grocery store. Churches may meet in movie theaters, local high schools, or homes. Some people may even choose to gather online for worship.

The COVID-19 pandemic caused many church leaders to wrestle with the identity of the church when its members were not gathered in a physical space. Many churches added a streaming option for their services for the first time. Others used the technology they had already been using to expand their online engagement with those who worshiped online at home. While some reject the online church as a legitimate expression of worship, I have found it beautiful, especially when it remains centered on Jesus.

CULTIVATING AN ONLINE CONGREGATION

When our leadership team began to discuss online engagement during the first six months of the COVID-19 pandemic, I was hesitant. Church is an embodied, enfleshed, real-time, life-on-life gathering of people in a common space at a given time. We are the relational body of Christ, and we are only as strong as the relational bonds that hold us together.

My concerns began to pile up as we discussed what a virtual church might look like. I struggled to imagine how we would form Christian community with people online because it is too easy to hide our true selves when we are on digital devices. I worried that virtual churches will make it too easy for people to watch at home instead of making the short drive to an in-person gathering. I feared that online church would further embolden those who want to "empty the pews." I questioned the longevity of online engagement for those who might find another church's online presence more attractive, creating the unhealthy experience of virtual church hopping. I was concerned that a virtual church experience could deepen the "worshiper as spectator" mentality and potentially increase loneliness and social disconnection. I feared that the specter of consumerism built into social-media platforms would fight against the Spirit of Jesus. I easily imagined how an online church experience could become more homogeneous, less multicultural, and less socioeconomically diverse. Suffice it to say, I had a lot of concerns. So I began to pray. Then, two things happened.

First, during the early days of COVID-19, I began meeting people from all over the country who were connecting with our church online. I met them in the small groups I hosted during the strictest time of the lockdown, when our church was only online. I didn't meet religious consumers. I met genuine followers of Jesus who called our church "home," people who longed for authentic community.

Second, my questioning in prayer began to change from *God, how are we going to overcome the obstacle of online engagement?* to *God, what are you doing among these people gathering online?* When I began to sense God's work among our "onliners" (our affectionate term for those who would become a part of our online congregation), my heart slowly began to open to these people and my thinking began to change. After about four months of online church, we officially opened membership to our online congregation.

I still have concerns about cultivating an online congregation, but then I always have concerns about the church. I'm a pastor, after all! I can relate to the apostle Paul, who wrote, "I am under daily pressure because of my anxiety for all the churches" (2 Corinthians 11:28). While I carry some anxiety about our online congregation, I cannot deny the fruit I have seen in the lives of our onliners. More than one of them has communicated to me that if they did not have this space to connect, they would have completely walked away from the faith. Others have expressed that they have discovered God's love revealed in Jesus Christ in new ways. I have spent one-on-one time with onliners, walking them through marriage difficulties, the stress of raising teenagers, a cancer diagnosis, and a myriad of theological challenges to their spiritual growth. Some of our onliners have acknowledged that they are isolated and our online congregation has become a lifeline for them. I still would prefer for our onliners to find a local in-person congregation (and some have). We offer online engagement as a concession, but it is a concession of mercy in the way of Jesus.

COVENANT TOGETHERNESS HELD TOGETHER BY JESUS

We are invited by Jesus to be part of what he has been doing, what he is doing, and what he will continue to do—building his church. Yes, church life can bring disappointments. Yes, we make mistakes. Yes, we try and fail and get back up again. Yes, people within the church will disappoint us. The church Jesus is building is marred and riddled with holes, but it is front and center in God's work on earth. Church is where we reject the individualism of our culture for what pastor and author Tara Beth Leach calls "covenant togetherness." She writes:

> The Christian life is not a solo journey; instead it is a journey of covenant togetherness. . . . Throughout the story of God, we don't see a vision for private pietism but holy

people. Sure, it's messy and flawed, but that's the beauty
of covenant togetherness. The church is filled with broken
sinners who often struggle to get along, agree, and see eye
to eye. And yet the same church is invited to *be the light* in a
dark, broken, and weary world.[2]

The beauty of Christian community is that we do not simply go
to church to hang out with our friends, loving those who love us.
Rather, we find ourselves with people whom we wouldn't necessarily
choose to spend time with, except that Jesus has brought us together
into a new family. What holds us together as a family is Jesus himself.

Jesus, the ruling and reigning Lamb of God, is at the center of this
new family he is calling together, and he is the head. Paul writes, "He
put all things under his feet and gave him as head over all things to
the church, which is his body, the fullness of him who fills all in all"
(Ephesians 1:22-23, ESV). As brothers and sisters in Jesus, we are the
body, but he is the head. Through his ascension, Jesus is the one who
"fills all things everywhere with himself" (Ephesians 1:23, NLT), and
he is doing so through the church. We do not set aside our participation in the church because Jesus has filled all things with himself.
Rather, we fully participate in the church because we are his body in
the world. Our task is to keep Jesus at the center. How do we do this?
I suggest five ways. We are centering Jesus in our worship life together
when Jesus is . . .

1. *proclaimed* through the Christian calendar;
2. *modeled and taught* in the lives of his people;
3. *celebrated* in Holy Communion;
4. *seen in one another* in sacred community; and
5. *reflected* into the world through acts of justice.

Let's look at each of these in turn.

Jesus proclaimed

The gospel we hear preached will determine the shape of the church we experience. The gospel itself is about Jesus. It's the bold announcement that Jesus is the Savior, Lord, and King of the whole world. In the saving reign of Jesus, we experience peace with God, forgiveness of sins, and healing for bodies and souls. And we receive the collective call to be the people of God proclaiming this good news, worshiping in a community of Jesus followers and cooperating with God in acts of justice. We need the proclamation of the gospel if people are to enter the Kingdom. We also need the ongoing proclamation of the gospel for staying in the Kingdom, focused on the Lamb of God as King.

One way we proclaim the gospel, the story of Jesus, is by participating in the church calendar, with its rhythm of liturgical seasons. The Christian calendar tells and retells the story of Jesus from Advent to Pentecost, from preparation for Jesus' birth and anticipating his return to the outpouring of the Spirit on the church, the body of Christ. Author Bobby Gross has described the annual Christian calendar as a Christ-centered dance:

> In devoting ourselves to Jesus, over time, our stories conform to his Story, our lives to his Life. From him we learn the waiting that enlarges, the giving that enriches and the telling that enlightens. With him we experience the turning that blessedly humbles us, the dying to self that leads to healing and the rising that heartens our whole being. And in pouring out ourselves like him, we receive his transforming power. This is the Christ-centered choreography of the Christian year.[3]

Observing the Christian calendar allows us to proclaim the story of Jesus in a way that allows us to find ourselves in that story. We have a calendar by which we set appointments and schedule events with our family and friends. This calendar begins in January. The Christian calendar begins four weeks before Christmas and continues for approximately six months until we arrive at Pentecost, where we remember the outpouring of the Spirit, empowering the church to walk in the ways of Jesus. The second half of the calendar is Ordinary Time, when we follow Jesus during "ordinary" weeks and months. Each of the seasons of the Christian calendar emphasize a particular part of Jesus' story, and then in Ordinary Time we live out the story of the people of God.

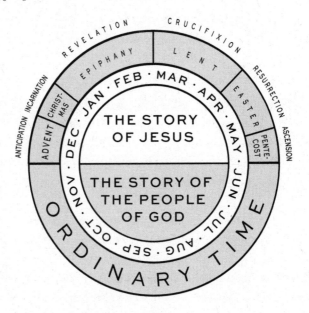

Most American Christians are familiar with Christmas and Easter because these holidays remain dominant in American culture. Some of the other holy days and seasons may be known by name, but their significance is unknown. Once followers of Jesus understand the meaning behind these traditions, the seasons become much more valuable in proclaiming Jesus in our worship gatherings. Here is a brief overview of each of the major seasons.[4]

- *Advent* is marked by a joyful spirit of anticipation, preparation, and longing. During Advent we wait for Jesus to come. We prepare for the celebration of the birth of Jesus the Christ in his first advent, and we live with the anticipation of the return of Jesus the King in his second advent. We mark Advent by the four Sundays before Christmas to remind ourselves that December is about so much more than Christmas parties and presents; it's about waiting for Jesus' coming. Advent is how we prepare for Christmas.

- *Christmas* isn't just one day! On the Christian calendar, it is a twelve-day celebration beginning on December 25.[5] We celebrate Christmas by giving gifts to friends and family to reflect the ultimate gift God gave us—Jesus, the Lamb of God. We celebrate and reflect on the moment in time when God came to us as a baby wrapped in swaddling clothes, a moment we call the Incarnation. As Bobby Gross explains, "If Advent is a season of waiting, Christmas is a season of wonder."[6] Often the Christmas celebration begins on Christmas Eve with candlelight and Communion.

- *Epiphany* marks the end of Christmas on January 6. We remember several important events in the life of Jesus during this season, including the visit of the wise men, who came to worship Jesus. This visit was a sign that Jesus would be the King of all people. We also remember Jesus' baptism and his first miracle. Epiphany is about God's act of revealing himself to the non-Jewish world.

- *Lent* is a forty-day season focused on Jesus' journey to Jerusalem that led to his suffering and death. Lent is a time to reflect on our own lives, remembering Jesus and repenting of things in our lives that do not reflect his ways. Lent includes fasting, a voluntary giving up of certain things, to remind us of the sufferings of Jesus. Just as Advent prepares us for Christmas, Lent prepares us for

Easter. We cannot fully experience the joy of Easter without the sorrow of Lent. There are multiple important days in this season.

- *Ash Wednesday*, the first day of Lent, is a day of prayer, fasting, and repentance. Often Christians have ashes applied to their foreheads at an Ash Wednesday service as a sign of humility and repentance.

- *Holy Week* is the week leading up to Easter, beginning on Palm Sunday (in liturgical traditions) or on the Monday after Palm Sunday (in some nonliturgical traditions).

- *Palm Sunday* is the Sunday before Easter, when we remember Jesus' entrance into Jerusalem before his death. We join the crowds to celebrate that the King has come, but we also weep with Jesus, knowing his death is coming soon.

- *Maundy Thursday* is the Thursday of Holy Week. We remember Jesus' last supper with his disciples. It's during this meal that Jesus gave us the mandate to love one another (John 13:34-36).

- *Good Friday* is the Friday of Holy Week. We remember the crucifixion of Jesus. It is at the cross where we most clearly see the cosuffering and self-giving love of God.

- *Holy Saturday* is the Saturday of Holy Week. We remember the death of Jesus. He died a real human death and lay lifeless in the tomb all day. This is the final day in the season of Lent.

- *Easter Sunday* is the ultimate day of Christian celebration. In one sense, we celebrate the Resurrection every Sunday, but after forty days of reflecting on Jesus' suffering, Easter begins our time of celebration like none other!

- *Eastertide* is the season of Easter when we continue to celebrate the resurrection of Jesus and his triumph over sin, death, and evil. Eastertide lasts fifty days.

- *Ascension Day* commemorates Jesus' ascension to the right hand of the Father forty days after his resurrection. The ascension isn't about Jesus going away but about his promotion to a position of authority over all things in heaven and earth. While Ascension Day is the sixth Thursday of Easter, it is often recognized on the following Sunday.

- *Pentecost Sunday* closes the Easter season on a day when we remember the Holy Spirit, who is the Spirit of Jesus. God poured the Holy Spirit on the church so that we could be fully empowered as the living, breathing body of Jesus on earth.

- *Ordinary Time* is the season after Pentecost. Here we continue to follow Jesus in our ordinary lives.

- *Christ the King Sunday*, the last Sunday before Advent, marks the end of Ordinary Time and the close of the Christian year.

When we observe these holy days and seasons, we tell the story of Jesus—and are formed as the people of Jesus—throughout the year. The Christian calendar focuses our attention on Jesus as we worship him from Advent to Christ the King Sunday.

Jesus modeled and taught

We proclaim Jesus in many ways in our life of worship together, including observing the Christian calendar. We also work at centering Jesus when we model and teach his ways to others. Jesus himself commissioned us with these words: "Go therefore and make disciples of all nations, baptizing them in the name of the Father and of the Son and of the Holy Spirit, and *teaching them to obey everything* that I have commanded you" (Matthew 28:19-20, emphasis added). We proclaim and teach the gospel because Jesus as King is a proclamation to be obeyed.[7] We cannot proclaim Jesus as King, the world's true ruler, and then not do what he says. To do so would be hypocritical. Jesus asked, "Why do you call me 'Lord, Lord,' and do not do what I tell you?" (Luke 6:46). Such hypocrisy prompts the strongest critique from Jesus. As I have written elsewhere, Christianity at its core is about living a life that reflects the way of Jesus.[8] We believe Jesus is the way, the only way, to the Father. And Jesus *is* the way to a full, abundant life—the good life we all seek.

The work of the church is making disciples. Everything we do, from worshiping together to serving the poor, works to form us as followers of Jesus. We don't have a discipleship program as much as we are a disciple-making people. We have sermons, books, classes, workshops, retreats, seminars, and small groups to teach the way of Jesus, but newer Christians also need to see it modeled in the lives of less-new Christians. In Romans 12, Paul exhorts us to recognize that we are one body in Christ (Romans 12:5). Within that one body we need seasoned saints who can embody a love that is genuine. We need people who imitate the Lamb of God, people who will "hate what is evil" and "hold fast to what is good" (Romans 12:9). The church with Jesus at the center models lives faithful to Paul's exhortation:

> Love one another with mutual affection; outdo one another
> in showing honor. Do not lag in zeal, be ardent in spirit,
> serve the Lord. Rejoice in hope, be patient in suffering,
> persevere in prayer. Contribute to the needs of the saints;
> extend hospitality to strangers.
> ROMANS 12:10-13

Jesus celebrated

The celebration of Holy Communion, or the Lord's Supper, is at the heart of Christian worship. Just as we make ourselves present to God through prayer, so also God makes the very life of the Holy Trinity present to us through Communion. Jesus described himself as the "bread from heaven" (John 6:32) and said, "My flesh is true food, and my blood is true drink. Whoever feeds on my flesh and drinks my blood abides in me, and I in him" (John 6:55-56, ESV). With these words Jesus establishes what we know as the celebration of Communion. We commune with him through the bread and the cup. Paul writes, "The cup of blessing that we bless, is it not a participation in the blood of Christ? The bread that we break, is it not a participation in the body of Christ?" (1 Corinthians 10:16, ESV). We are centering Jesus in our worship life together when we keep Holy Communion in a central place in our time of worship.

My heart longs to meet Jesus at the Communion table, and that longing has not decreased even as I practice Communion weekly. In his sermon "The Duty of Constant Communion," John Wesley encouraged Christians to participate in Holy Communion as often as they could to experience God's mercy. Wesley asked:

> Why do you not accept of his mercy as often as ever you can? God now offers you his blessing; — why do you refuse it? You have now an opportunity of receiving his mercy; — why do you not receive it? You are weak: — why do not you seize every opportunity of increasing your strength?[9]

Some claim that if we practice Communion too often it will lose some of its sacredness, but that has not been my experience. I tell my wife every day that I love her, and this repetition has not diminished the sacredness of our relationship. Perhaps we should celebrate Jesus through the Lord's Supper as often as we say "I love you." I have the privilege of not only receiving Communion weekly but also serving the Elements of Communion to others nearly every Sunday. More than once tears have filled my eyes as I offer the cup to a member of our church with the words, "The blood of Christ shed for you." As I share those words with people in my congregation, I am often overwhelmed by God's mercy. During the experience of Communion, I am renewed in my confidence that Jesus is the saving King. Our loving response to the gospel includes our participation in Holy Communion. God is indeed saving the world, and we acknowledge this when we eat and drink at the Communion table.

Different churches follow different traditions of how—and how often—Communion is practiced. Whatever this looks like in your church, Communion is how we "proclaim the Lord's death until he comes" (1 Corinthians 11:26). As we receive the Lord's Supper, we proclaim Jesus' great sacrifice for us. And every time we eat the bread and drink the cup, we celebrate this sacrifice with humility and reverence.

Jesus seen in one another

The beauty of Christian community is that God is creating a new family of people united by their love for—and faith in—Jesus. This new family breaks down walls erected between racial groups, genders, and socioeconomic classes.

The words *community* and *family* describe the church well. Church isn't merely an idea. It is the interconnected relationships of people: real people, fallible people, different kinds of people. The challenge of community is learning to love people who aren't like us, and out of this challenge comes deep formation in the ways of Jesus.

Learning to love one another requires seeing and valuing the differences we bring to the community—and also seeing Jesus in one another. We each have unconsciously developed the habit of meeting someone new and then silently categorizing them. In Christian community we keep Jesus at the center when we welcome new people into the community, seeing their faith and how that faith is shaping the image of Jesus in their hearts.

Jesus invites us into Christian community so that through our relationships with others we can strip off our old selves and put on our new selves, renewed in the image of God. Paul writes, "put off your old self, which belongs to your former manner of life and is corrupt through deceitful desires, and . . . be renewed in the spirit of your minds, and . . . put on the new self, created after the likeness of God in true righteousness and holiness" (Ephesians 4:22-24, ESV). As together we find ourselves in a process of putting on the "new self," we begin to see Jesus in one another. Paul continues in Ephesians 4 to describe the fundamental practices that build the community and enable us to see Jesus in one another:

- speaking the truth to one another (verse 25);
- keeping anger from growing into sin (verses 26-27);
- working hard and sharing with anyone in need (verse 28);
- speaking in a way that builds up, giving grace to those who hear (verse 29);
- putting away bitterness, anger, and slander (verse 31); and
- being kind to and forgiving one another (verse 32).

Regularly practicing these things will keep Jesus at the center of the church and will train us to recognize Jesus in one another.

Jesus reflected

The local church with the Lamb of God at the center reflects Jesus into the world, cooperating with God in the work of Jesus. Tara Beth Leach reminds us, "A radiant church reflects the radiant image of God—Jesus. Jesus is the *radiance* of God's glory, and the church reflects the *radiance* of Jesus."[10] Jesus came as "the reflection of God's glory and the exact imprint of God's very being" (Hebrews 1:3). Jesus perfectly reflects God's image, and our task is to reflect Jesus' image into the world. In Christian vocabulary, that reflection manifests as justice. When we advocate for justice or serve the needs in our neighborhoods, we are reflecting Jesus into God's good world. Doing justice is how we love our neighbor in tangible ways.

As people continue to reject the local church and walk away from regular participation in it, we have an opportunity to demonstrate the significance of gathering in worship by centering Jesus in our common life of worship. Adopting the Christian calendar with its seasons and traditions allows us to tell and retell the story of Jesus every year. We can demonstrate Jesus' life as we love one another in community. We can celebrate Jesus every time we come to the Lord's Table. We can look for Jesus in one another and then, when we are scattered into our neighborhoods, workplaces, and schools, we can reflect the life of Jesus by doing justice. Let's turn our attention to this monumental task in the next chapter.

DISCUSSION QUESTIONS

1. What is your first memory of a church gathering? How old were you? What do you recall about that initial experience?

2. What are the challenges with an online-only experience of church? What is the value in it?

3. What has been your experience with the Christian calendar with its liturgical seasons?

4. Who in your life has modeled the way of Jesus to you?

5. How is Communion celebrated in your church? How do you keep Communion sacred and special?

6. How have your connections at church helped you grow in faith?

7. How should we respond when we do not rightly reflect Jesus in the world?

8. Which of these five practices—Jesus proclaimed, Jesus modeled and taught, Jesus celebrated, Jesus seen in others, Jesus reflected—do you need to give attention to?

JUSTICE IN THE PEACEABLE KINGDOM OF GOD

Keep, O Lord, your household the Church in your steadfast
faith and love, that through your grace we may proclaim
your truth with boldness, and minister your justice with
compassion; for the sake of our Savior Jesus Christ, who
lives and reigns with you and the Holy Spirit, one God, now
and for ever. Amen.

A COLLECT, PROPER 6,
THE BOOK OF COMMON PRAYER

OVER TIME THE church in North America has become divided
over matters of justice because Christians don't always emphasize the
same implications of redemption. Conservative, evangelical churches
have tended to focus more on the individual, personal effects of God's
work of redemption, like forgiveness of sin and personal transformation. Progressive, mainline churches have tended to focus more on
the communal, public effects of redemption, like social reform and
serving the poor. With this unfortunate divide, mainline Protestant
churches and segments of the Catholic church have primarily been
the torchbearers for God's work of justice in the earth. The truth is
we need to emphasize both the personal and the public expressions
of God's redemptive acts because both personal salvation and social
justice are a part of what Jesus is doing with his Kingdom. Justice
belongs to the whole body of Christ.

Consider how the prophet Jeremiah weaves together both themes. Speaking of a coming new covenant, Jeremiah prophesied:

> This is the covenant that I will make with the house of Israel after those days, says the LORD: I will put my law within them, and *I will write it on their hearts*; and I will be their God, and they shall be my people. No longer shall they teach one another, or say to each other, "Know the LORD," for *they shall all know me*, from the least of them to the greatest, says the LORD; for *I will forgive their iniquity*, and remember their sin no more.
> JEREMIAH 31:33-34, EMPHASIS ADDED

God's new covenant will include experiences we associate with personal salvation—God's activity in our hearts, intimate knowledge of God, and forgiveness of sins. Later the word of the Lord came again to Jeremiah, and he uttered these words:

> The days are surely coming, says the LORD, when I will fulfill the promise I made to the house of Israel and the house of Judah. In those days and at that time I will cause a righteous Branch to spring up for David; and *he shall execute justice* and righteousness in the land. In those days Judah will be saved and Jerusalem will live in safety. And this is the name by which it will be called: "The LORD is our righteousness."
> JEREMIAH 33:14-16, EMPHASIS ADDED

God's new covenant will also include God's work of justice in the land. In God's new creation project, God not only sets right his people, he also intends to set right his good world. To progressive Christians, Jeremiah says, "God's new covenant includes the forgiveness of sins and the personal knowledge of God." To conservative Christians, Jeremiah says, "New covenant theology includes Jesus' work of executing justice and righteousness in the earth." Justice does not belong to certain Christians. It belongs to all who worship Jesus as the slain Lamb.

Regrettably, issues surrounding social justice have become so politicized in the United States that it has become difficult for followers of Jesus to initiate conversations about justice without being vilified by one political group or another. The cry for justice remains controversial for those who associate justice with a plank in a political platform. Years ago I heard a popular conservative political commentator warn people of faith that if their churches talked about justice, then they should leave immediately because the term *social justice* is code language. While he didn't clarify what the term was code for, he implied that it somehow indicated a left-leaning political agenda. I can understand how a political pundit with little biblical understanding could mistake the language of justice for a political ideology, but the reality is justice is not only language used by politicians; it is also language spoken by the church.

Justice belongs to the ancient Christian faith. Standing on the foundation of the Hebrew prophets before him, Jesus criticized the Pharisees for their legalistic and hypocritical religious practices. Jesus said, "Woe to you, scribes and Pharisees, hypocrites! For you tithe mint, dill, and [cumin], and have neglected the weightier matters of the law: justice and mercy and faith. It is these you ought to have practiced without neglecting the others" (Matthew 23:23). God gave the Mosaic law to the children of Abraham to form them into a people marked by worship and justice. The law directed Israel to love God (worship) and love neighbor (justice). Jesus associated justice with the "weightier matters" of the Jewish law, a law that has been fulfilled in Jesus himself. Now that we have been set free from the letter of the law, we follow Jesus, living in harmony with the spirit of the law by loving God through acts of worship and loving our neighbors through acts of justice.

TOWARD A BIBLICAL DEFINITION OF JUSTICE

One afternoon when I was pastoring in rural south Georgia, I found myself in a conversation with a Black pastor about the possibility and viability of reparations for slavery. I had a very immature vision of justice when I was in my early thirties when this conversation occurred. Growing up in a predominantly white, middle-class, midwestern American environment shaped my imagination to see justice in terms of law enforcement. The messages I had received growing up in a predominantly white community had scripted me to believe justice was a matter of the good guys catching the bad guys and putting them in jail. Certainly justice includes the enforcement of just laws, but I have come to discover that God's justice is far more than *criminal* justice. Early on in my years as a pastor, though, I had not yet come to understand the depths of God's justice.

We discussed reparations respectfully, though I suspect that neither of us had much knowledge on the subject. The other pastor argued that the US government had a moral obligation to pay the descendants of slaves for the economic injustice of slavery. I was following his logic until he added "because of what *your* people did."

I responded as honestly as I could. I explained to him that my ancestry is Dutch. My ancestors were living in the Netherlands in the eighteenth and nineteenth centuries. My family didn't emigrate to the United States until the early 1900s.

He replied, "Good point."

While we did not resolve anything in that conversation, we did hear one another.

That conversation revealed many things to me, including that justice is deeply complex. Issues of justice require context and the ability to see another person's perspective. It was years after that conversation before I began to see the experience of racial injustice from the perspective of a Black man living in America. This conversation also revealed that justice is often tied to both politics and economics, which is to say that justice is connected to power and money and thus is infused with controversy. I don't pretend to have the solutions to the problems of misaligned power and economic inequality. But as I follow Jesus I cannot escape the call to work toward racial justice in the church to serve as a model for racial justice in our world.

Before we imagine Jesus as the Lamb of God at the center of our engagement in justice, we need a shared understanding of what justice is. I appreciate theologian Chris Marshall's insight on the dilemma of defining *justice*: "We all know that justice is important, we all feel obligated towards the demands of justice, we all sense the primordial pull of justice. But we cannot say exactly what justice is, or how best to define it."[1]

Since justice belongs to the Christian faith, let's start by looking for a working definition in our sacred and inspired text. The word *justice* appears around 130 times in the NRSV. While it only appears 14 times in the New Testament, we come across it over 100 times in the Old Testament. The Hebrew word most often translated "justice" is *mišpāt* (pronounced "mish-pot"), and it takes on a variety of meanings depending on the context, including "God's intended order for His creation"[2] and "the way of living under the judgments that have been made."[3] Consider this passage from Deuteronomy:

> For the LORD your God is God of gods and Lord of lords, the great, the mighty, and the awesome God, who is not partial and takes no bribe. He executes justice [*mišpāt*] for the fatherless and the widow, and loves the sojourner, giving him food and clothing. Love the sojourner, therefore, for you were sojourners in the land of Egypt.
> DEUTERONOMY 10:17-19, ESV

In this passage we see justice (*mišpāt*) connected with:

* God's actions;
* equity for those who have less;
* doing what is right; and
* moral laws for God's people to follow.

Consider another passage from Deuteronomy:

> You shall not pervert the justice [*mišpāt*] due to the
> sojourner or to the fatherless, or take a widow's garment
> in pledge, but you shall remember that you were a slave in
> Egypt and the LORD your God redeemed you from there;
> therefore I command you to do this.
>
> When you reap your harvest in your field and forget
> a sheaf in the field, you shall not go back to get it. It
> shall be for the sojourner, the fatherless, and the widow,
> that the LORD your God may bless you in all the work
> of your hands.
> DEUTERONOMY 24:17-19, ESV

In this passage we see justice (*mišpāt*) connected with:

* God's covenant relationship with his people;
* human rights / one's "just due";
* generosity; and
* power dynamics.

Justice is also fundamentally relational. In addition to *mišpāt*, the concept of justice in the Old Testament is also connected with the Hebrew word *sᵉdāqâ* (pronounced "se-da-kah"), often translated "righteousness." In fact, the words sometimes appear together. For example, "The LORD is exalted, for he dwells on high; he will fill Zion with justice [*mišpāt*] and righteousness [*sᵉdāqâ*]" (Isaiah 33:5, ESV). While *sᵉdāqâ* and *mišpāt* are twin concepts with a lot of overlap, *sᵉdāqâ* emphasizes the relational and interpersonal part of justice.[4] Righteousness is the experience of living rightly within the context of a covenantal relationship. While modern Christians tend to think of a relationship with God as personal and individual, the ancient people of God experienced their relationship with God communally. The ancient covenants were between God and his people *as a community*. The righteousness God wants to pour out in the world is a rightness embodied in community.

God loves these twin concepts—righteousness and justice. This is evident from the Scriptures. "For the word of the LORD is upright," we read in Psalm 33, "and all his work is done in faithfulness. He loves righteousness and justice; the earth is full of the steadfast love of the LORD" (Psalm 33:4-5). In fact, righteousness and justice flow from God's love. Everything we say about who God is and what God does is built on that foundation. Nothing is more basic to our understanding of God than this—God is love. The divine nature we are invited to participate in is love (2 Peter 1:4).

Justice and righteousness typify who God is and how God rules and reigns. Psalm 89 explains: "Righteousness and justice are the foundation of your throne; steadfast love and faithfulness go before you" (Psalm 89:14). Biblical justice advocate Jessica Nicholas shares, "In every step of God's plan, justice and righteousness are essential. They are foundational to His throne and central to how He reigns, so it makes sense that they characterize everything He does, and that He requires His people to follow His ways."[5] For us to participate in this divine love, we must also pursue righteousness and justice.

JESUS AND JUSTICE

Jesus came with a mission defined in terms of justice. As the full embodiment of Israel's God, Jesus carried forth Israel's mission to be a light to the nations, and he brought with him the justice and righteousness God loves. He came as a fulfillment of Israel's prophets, who claimed as much. "Behold, the days are coming, declares the LORD," Jeremiah wrote, "when I will raise up for David a righteous Branch, and he shall reign as king and deal wisely, and shall execute *justice* and *righteousness* in the land" (Jeremiah 23:5, ESV, emphasis added). Isaiah prophesied (and Matthew echoed him): "Here is my servant, whom I have chosen, my beloved, with whom my soul is well pleased. I will put my Spirit upon him, and he will proclaim justice to the Gentiles" (Matthew 12:18). Jesus gives us a picture of the result once justice has completed its work, which is the experience of life—the good life, abundant life, eternal life—and Jesus is how we do justice.

The center of our work toward and advocacy for justice is Jesus as the Lamb of God. The justice-oriented tasks of each Jesus follower will differ. The beauty implicit in the diversity of the body of Christ is that we find our hearts drawn to different justice callings.

Pastor and author Rich Villodas roots our desire to advocate for particular needs in the burdens we carry. "We all have particular parts to play in God's redemptive plan," he explains, "and these parts are often discerned through the burdens we carry for a particular people, issue, or call."[6] Some of us advocate for the poor and those living in substandard housing. Some of us advocate for refugees and the plight of immigrants struggling for citizenship. Some of us advocate for the unborn and young pregnant women in need of help. Some of us advocate for racial justice, at-risk youth, or domestic-abuse victims. Our advocacy may not look the same, but it comes from the same place of love, with Jesus at the heart of it.

Without Jesus at the center of our practice of justice, it's too easy for us to give into rage and retaliation. As pastor and author Derwin Gray points out, *"Justice without Jesus is vengeance.* God's mercy is for the oppressor *and* the oppressed."[7] Jesus taught us the way of enemy love because God wants to rescue both the oppressed and the oppressor. The gift of the age to come is for both the powerful and the powerless. In the age to come "the wolf shall live with the lamb, the leopard shall lie down with the kid" (Isaiah 11:6). Jesus offers us that life now. If both the powerful and the powerless will turn to the Lamb, who takes away the sin of the world and provides healing and mercy for all, both can experience redemption. The peaceableness we imagine, where predators and prey live together without fear, is a picture of the life of the age to come. Because we live at the overlap of the ages, we can begin to experience that peace now.[8] And it starts with centering Jesus in how we think about justice.

Injustice can often provoke a variety of emotions, including grief, fear, and anger. Feeling things like disgust and anger at the sight of injustice is a normal and justifiable human response to others' suffering. However, *unresolved* anger that we allow to settle deep into our bones can, over time, devolve into bitterness, rage, hate, and violence. Paul advises us to jettison those soul-crushing weights: "Put away from you all bitterness and wrath and anger and wrangling and slander, together with all malice" (Ephesians 4:31). We get rid of those things because we are being renewed (Ephesians 4:23). As we have seen, we are stripping off our old self and putting on a "new self, created according to the likeness of God in true righteousness and holiness" (Ephesians 4:24). Our new self, which is free of bitterness, rage, and anger, reflects the true nature of God, who is love and mercy.[9]

Anger can be a powerful motivator. Rage and hate of oppressors can produce results, but justice in the name of hate is not justice in the way of Jesus. What do we do with anger over injustice? First we follow the lead of many of the Psalms and we bring that anger into

God's presence. We offer prayers with lament in our hearts and words on our lips like these:

> How long, O LORD? Will you forget me forever?
>   How long will you hide your face from me?
> How long must I bear pain in my soul,
>   and have sorrow in my heart all day long?
> How long shall my enemy be exalted over me?
> PSALM 13:1-2

We bring our anger into God's presence and, through prayers of lament, we leave that anger there. Once we are free of anger, we look for tangible ways to work for justice in our world. When we are centering Jesus in our work for justice, we labor from a position of love and mercy. When we commit ourselves to work for justice in the way of the Lamb, we will encounter resistance and misunderstanding, and we could experience suffering. We will be tempted to retaliate, to return insult for insult and hate for hate. We can consider ourselves blessed to have women and men who have gone before us, Jesus-centered justice advocates who walked in his way. We can learn from how they lived. The story of one such life will take us on a trip to rural Mississippi.

JOHN PERKINS'S STORY

Born in poverty in the 1930s as the son of a Black sharecropper, John Perkins grew up on a cotton plantation as a Black child in a world where racial animosity dominated the culture. His mother died, and his father took him to live with his grandmother. As a teenager he lost his brother Clyde, a decorated World War II veteran. Clyde was shot and killed by a white member of law enforcement.

John continued to be harassed, experiencing not only the trauma of the loss of his mother, the absence of his father, and the murder of his brother but also the ongoing trauma of segregation and oppression in the American South. After Clyde's death, John moved to California in search of hope and healing. In 1951 he married Vera Mae and they started a family. John worked in a local grocery store and began to experience economic stability and the love of a growing family.

In 1957, John heard a sermon based on Galatians 2:20. John later described it as the moment that he wanted to know God: "That day I really believed that he loved me. If there's a God who loves me enough to give his only begotten Son then that really is good news. . . . This God was willing to give his son for me! I had heard before that Jesus had died, but never that he had died for me."[10] John's newfound faith in Jesus caused him to experience God's love and become awakened to the dignity given to all of us by God. He would grow to see the gospel as the message of God's rescuing and redeeming love for all people, a love that could change lives and communities torn apart by hate and violence. John explained, "He saves us from our sin and the wounds and damage of sin, and that for me turned into gratitude. We love him because he first loves us, and that's where my energy comes from. Before, I didn't have purpose."[11]

John and his family returned to Mississippi in 1960 to proclaim the gospel that had changed the course of his life. He chose Mendenhall, in between Jackson and Hattiesburg, as a base for an evangelistic ministry. As the civil rights movement of the 1960s began to capture the attention of white and Black Americans, John lent his voice to speak out against the racial injustices he saw and experienced. In the fall of 1969, John led an economic boycott of white-owned stores in Mendenhall. On February 7, 1970, following the arrest of students who had taken part in a protest march in Mendenhall, John was arrested and tortured by white police officers. In his 1976 biography, *Let Justice Roll Down,* John recalls the hate he felt for his oppressors as he lay in bed recovering:

> I began to see with horror how hate could destroy me—destroy me more devastatingly and suddenly than any destruction I could bring on those who had wronged me. I could try and fight back, as many of my brothers had done. But if I did, how would I be different from the whites who hate?
>
> And where would hating get me? Anyone can hate. This whole business of hating and hating back. It's what keeps the vicious circle of racism going.
>
> The Spirit of God worked on me as I lay in that bed. An image formed in my mind. The image of the cross—Christ on the cross. It blotted out everything else in my mind.
>
> This Jesus knew what I had suffered. He understood. And He cared. Because He had experienced it all Himself.
>
> This Jesus, this One who had brought good news directly from God in heaven, had lived what He preached. Yet He was arrested and falsely accused. Like me, He went through an unjust trial. He also faced a lynch mob and got beaten. But even more than that, He was nailed to rough wooden planks and killed. Killed like a common criminal.
>
> At the crucial moment, it seemed to Jesus that even God Himself had deserted Him. The suffering was so great, He cried out in agony. He was dying.
>
> But when He looked at that mob that had lynched Him, He didn't hate them. He loved them. He forgave them. And He prayed God to forgive them. "Father, forgive these people, for they don't know what they are doing."
>
> His enemies hated. But Jesus forgave. I couldn't get away from that. . . .

It's a profound, mysterious truth—Jesus' concept of love overpowering hate. I may not see its victory in my lifetime. But I know it's true.

I know it's true, because it happened to me. On that bed, full of bruises and stitches—God made it true in me. He washed my hatred away and replaced it with a love for the white man in rural Mississippi.

I felt strong again. Stronger than ever. What doesn't destroy me makes me stronger.

I know it's true.

Because it happened to me.[12]

The inhumane brutality John experienced that night could have formed his heart in hate and revenge, but hate could find no foothold. In a beautiful act of redemption, John went on to champion racial justice and reconciliation, launching ministries and organizations to express God's love for all people.

Racial justice is one area of justice for which all Christians can advocate. It is particularly central to the work of Jesus because the church Jesus is building is a large multiethnic family. Rich Villodas describes the flourishing of a multiethnic church as one of the main purposes of the gospel.[13] Those who gather around the throne to sing "Worthy is the Lamb" are not just those who have been redeemed from one race of people, but "saints from every tribe and language and people and nation" (Revelation 5:9). Sadly not all Christians value this purpose of the gospel.

Advocating for racial justice will not make everyone in the church happy, which is a helpful reminder that peacemaking in the way of Jesus is not an attempt to get everyone to like us. Advocating for justice will inevitably make some people uncomfortable. It will be offensive to some. Giving voice to the systemic oppression of people of color in the United States will create offense among some white

Christians. Yet we cannot allow the fear of offense to prevent us from advocating for justice in our prayers and in our actions. Peacemaking requires patience. It takes time for white Christians to see and feel the ongoing suffering of brothers and sisters of color. It took me a long time. For years I couldn't see or understand the toll that centuries of racial prejudice had taken on Black and Brown Christians. Fortunately, Jesus' way of peace gives space for enemies to repent and become friends. I have sat in spaces where people of color have shared their stories of struggle and pain and white people have acknowledged their ignorance of Black oppression. Repentance for and rejection of white dominance is possible, but sadly, not everyone will see it. Not everyone will enter the lament of it and repent.

Justice-making in the way of Jesus will cause division because some people will refuse the way of love. Jesus himself wasn't loved by everyone. The poor loved him. The sick and sinners loved him. The humble in heart loved him. "Some argued, 'He's a good man,' but others said, 'He's nothing but a fraud who deceives the people'" (John 7:12, NLT). If we follow Jesus, we can expect the same treatment. As followers of the Lamb, we have no other choice than to start with loving peace. As we read in the Psalms, "Mark the blameless, and behold the upright, for there is posterity for the peaceable" (Psalm 37:37). I believe there *is* posterity for the peaceable. There is a future for the forgivers and a legacy from those who love. But like John Perkins, we must be willing to suffer discord when we lift our voices in the name of justice.

God loves justice and because we love God, we love what God loves. If we choose to practice racial justice in the way of the Lamb, there are at least four things we can do. First we can listen to the stories told by people of a different ethnicity. We don't need a theory to understand racial injustice; we just need to listen to a racially diverse group of people sharing their experiences. Second, bear the burdens of the racially oppressed. Don't brush off the reports of injustice you hear. Rather, feel their pain. Third, pray prayers of lament and cry out to God for justice. Part of our job in prayer is to sum up the suffering of God's good world and bring it into God's presence. Finally, advocate for justice publicly, in whatever arenas and capacities God moves you to. Having examined our role in working toward racial justice, let's turn our attention to political engagement, another arena in which followers of the Lamb must look to Jesus for a way forward.

DISCUSSION QUESTIONS

1. Have you participated in churches that emphasize the personal work of redemption (personal salvation) or the more public-oriented work of redemption (social justice)?

2. Why do we need an emphasis on both personal salvation and social justice as followers of Jesus?

3. In your own words, how would you describe God's work of justice?

4. What are the problems with engaging in justice from a place of bitterness, hate, or anger?

5. Describe a time when you witnessed racism, heard an account of racism experienced by another, or experienced racism yourself.

6. How can the church both advocate for racial justice and practice patience with those who prefer to ignore the topic?

7. What specific injustice(s) do you feel your heart drawn toward?

8. What can you do to advocate for justice in your community?

NOT A DONKEY OR AN ELEPHANT BUT A LAMB

Almighty and everlasting God, you govern all things both
in heaven and on earth: Mercifully hear the supplications of
your people, and in our time grant us your peace; through
Jesus Christ our Lord, who lives and reigns with you and the
Holy Spirit, one God, for ever and ever. Amen.

A COLLECT, FOURTH SUNDAY AFTER THE EPIPHANY,
THE BOOK OF COMMON PRAYER

TAKE A DEEP BREATH.

We are going to take a dive into political waters.

Politics has always been divisive. Today, many of us hold our political opinions so close to our self-identity that if we are challenged by an alternative political point of view, we feel personally attacked. Social media, as a political tool and outlet for political commentary, hasn't helped decrease the divisiveness or hostility. We have become polarized, divided into two warring tribes, us versus them. The division we experience from our political opinions is not with politics per se. The deeper issue is with how we engage in politics in the public square. The complete breakdown of civility in our political conversations brings to light the problems with how we communicate, how we listen, how we process emotions when we are tangled up in disagreement, how we process what we believe about social issues, and how we express our beliefs (which may or may not be in flux). By turning our attention to the Lamb of God, we can learn a way of truth telling that may not always bridge political gaps but can decrease hostility enough to turn bitter enemies into conversation partners.

The political clamor in American culture seems to reach a fever pitch during presidential election season. For some this four-year roller coaster has become a plunge into collective absurdity where social-media feeds once filled with pictures of kids and pets turn into nonstop political ads and debates about candidates. For others, an election season is the culmination of the frantic political wrangling by which they find their core identity. Political talk, arguments, and wars never really go away. While some people allow the waves of political clamoring to wash over them every day, others prefer to remain on the sandy beach, under an umbrella, dipping their feet into the political saltwater every four years. Very few of us can avoid these conversations for long.

I was born under the reign of Richard Nixon. I faintly remember critique of the Jimmy Carter administration, vividly remember Ronald Reagan and George H. W. Bush, and I reached voting age by the time of the 1992 presidential election. I've lived as an adult under Bill Clinton, George W. Bush, Barack Obama, Donald Trump, and Joe Biden. Their administrations each brought division and contention, but hostility during the Trump years generated an altogether different dynamic. Donald Trump's ascendancy in political power intensified the political divide and antagonism to an even higher level, particularly among followers of Jesus. In some segments of the American church, Christians applauded Trump for being "the most pro-life-friendly president in modern history."[1] Other Christians questioned Trump's character and competency. Some Christians appreciated his combative, tell-it-like-it-is style. Other Christians despised his rhetoric, his policies, and his social-media presence.

Trump's mode of political operation was driven not so much by a political ideology or by some vision of religiously informed morality. Trump based his political agenda on what works, as defined by the agenda he set. Trump was first and foremost a pragmatist who wanted to get the job done, which was clear from his political speeches and his social-media posts. He capitalized on getting things done by fighting those who disagreed with him. Trump's tone pleased some sincere followers of Jesus, and it infuriated others. Where Christians can agree is that his approach did enliven and motivate his political base. But it also deepened the divide and intensified the rage in our political discourse.

The verbal rage turned into physical rage on January 6, 2021, when a mob left a Washington DC Trump rally to storm into the United States Capitol Building. The mob had heard Trump and his allies contest the results of the 2020 election. The protestors at the Capitol Building soon overwhelmed Capitol Police. Once the outer barricades had been breached, the mob stormed into the Capitol. Members of Congress, the vice president, and other staffers were taken to a safe location, but in the end 140 people were injured, 5 people died, and many watched coverage of the event in disbelief and dismay.

In a video released on his Twitter account two hours after protestors had violently entered the Capitol Building, Trump said:

> I know your pain. I know you're hurt. We had an election that was stolen from us. It was a landslide election, and everyone knows it, especially the other side. But you have to go home now. We have to have peace. We have to have law and order. We have to respect our great people in law and order. We don't want anybody hurt.
>
> It's a very tough period of time. There's never been a time like this where such a thing happened where they could take it away from all of us—from me, from you, from our

country. This was a fraudulent election, but we can't play
into the hands of these people. We have to have peace. So
go home.

We love you. You're very special. You've seen what
happens. You see the way others are treated that are so bad
and so evil. I know how you feel, but go home, and go home
in peace.[2]

Even this statement divides Christians. Some followers of Jesus
applauded Trump's call for peace. Others agreed with Senate Minority
Leader Mitch McConnell, who noted Trump's false claim of a stolen
election made him "practically and morally responsible for provoking
the events of [that] day."[3] January 6, 2021, was a dark day in American
history. We witnessed the results of the ongoing churning of hostility
in popular American politics.

NEITHER TO THE LEFT NOR TO THE RIGHT

The reality is we live in a political world. The word *politics* is rooted
in the Greek word *polis*, meaning city. If we are going to live in a
city, whether it be a densely populated metropolitan urban area or a
one-red-light, sparsely populated rural town, we need some structure
in order to thrive. We cannot completely avoid politics because if we
intend to live as a society, and if we'd like for that society to flourish,
then we will have to learn how to live together. We need politics for
the polis.

As citizens of the Kingdom of God, Christians cannot avoid
politics, but we can avoid *partisan* politics. Partisanship is absolute
allegiance to one political party, ideology, or platform. Professor and
author Lee Camp describes Christian participation in partisanship as
a loss of Christian identity. When we become partisan, we have traded
our Christian birthright for a bowl of political soup. He writes:

The fundamental identity of American Christians, if Christianity means anything, is in being Christian, not in being American. And the fundamental role of the Christian community, to use the apostle's language, is to serve as a ministry of reconciliation, to serve as ministers of reconciliation to God and thereby to one another. To the degree that we fall prey to hysterics of partisanship, to that same degree have we lost our way as a Christian community.

Put differently, the partisan nature of Christianity in American politics is itself a denial of basic Christian political practices.[4]

The hostility of America's political climate makes it nearly impossible for Christians to affiliate completely with either party and retain their Christian identity. The politics of Jesus simply do not align totally with either the Democratic or the Republican platform. When Christians do try to align themselves with one political party, not only do they subjugate their core Christian political practices but they also allow the antagonism between donkeys and elephants to misshape their political imagination.

To promote the interests of one political party in the current climate of American politics nearly always requires a blind allegiance to that party's platform and ideology, allowing no room for dialogue, discussion, or nuanced consideration of the ideas of any other party. Once this lockstep allegiance to one political party begins to form our identity (how we think about ourselves) and shape our worldview (how we see and interpret the world), we begin to bend and flex our faith to fit neatly into our party's views.

The time has come for repentance because the Kingdom of God has come near. We need a renewed political imagination, one that rejects an allegiance to donkeys or elephants, one shaped by Jesus as the Lamb on the throne, whereby our political opinions and actions align with King Jesus and his administration. The politics of Jesus cannot be found somewhere in the center between the political left and right because the politics of King Jesus transcend those of fallen human beings. The time has come for Christians to unite not around a donkey or an elephant but a lamb. We renew our political imagination when we see the viability of the Kingdom of God as the politics of Jesus. But before we launch into a biblical understanding of the Kingdom of God, let me share a bit about my own understanding of politics.

MY POLITICAL JOURNEY

I grew up in a right-leaning home. I learned to value citizenship more than partisanship, and that we had a duty to remain politically aware, to vote, and to advocate for the common good. I became an intentional follower of Jesus in high school in a church that was aligned politically with the religious right. I remember very little political talk at that church, although my most active years there were between presidential election years. I went off to college in the fall of 1992 during the political campaigns of George H. W. Bush, Bill Clinton, and Ross Perot, who ran as an independent. I remember finding myself caught in a political debate in the student lounge of our dorm, arguing for the conservative economic policies of Bush, not necessarily because I had thought with any depth about the ramifications for the poor as a result of such policies but because I knew Bush was anti-abortion, and I had been scripted to believe Christians always vote "pro-life."

In the late 2000s, as a young pastor, I began to read essays from moral theologian Stanley Hauerwas and became convinced that the teachings of Jesus form a politic for Christians to live as a civic society. I'd come to believe that central to the politics of Jesus is the practice of nonviolence, which David Cramer and Myles Werntz describe as a core practice in Christian virtue.[5] I learned God's desire for the restoration and salvation of the world was not limited to individuals, but in how we as individuals live together. I began to see the gospel as the gospel of the Kingdom, where King Jesus has come (and will come again!) to make all things new. Since God intends on renewing our systems and structures, God begins by making us new. We become redeemed so that we can be what N. T. Wright calls "the justified justice-bringers" and "the reconciled reconcilers."[6] Today I have a political vision shaped by the tension between Anglican engagement and Anabaptist detachment, between active participation in the political process and separatist, nonparticipation in the political arena.

In my vacillating between political activism and quietism, I feel the dangerous seduction of proximity to political power, but I cannot completely pull back from all forms of political participation either because I've seen the harm created by unjust laws and immoral politicians. I find myself today in agreement with author Eugene Cho. He writes, "*Politics matter*. They matter because politics inform policies that ultimately impact people. When I read the Bible, it's emphatically clear that *people matter to God*."[7]

So politics do matter, but they have the potential to become an idol. The first sign of idolatry appears when we begin to rethink our understanding of the ways of Jesus to make them fit our political opinions. When our understanding of politics comes into direct conflict with the teachings of Jesus, something has to give. In this conflict, we face the temptation to run headlong into partisan politics and bow down to the idol of nationalism, the sin of loving our nation above all other loves—our love for God in particular.

This kind of politicization of the soul is a modern form of idolatry. In my own journey, I have come to find that the solution to polarization, division in the church, and political idolatry is to center Jesus in my political imagination. We experience this shaping of our imagination by pledging our allegiance, not to a donkey or an elephant but solely to the Lamb.

THE KINGDOM OF GOD AS THE POLITICS OF JESUS

King Jesus is political whether we like it or not; he is a king, after all. The language of *king* and *kingdom* sound rather archaic in our ears. Throughout the centuries the phrases *the Kingdom of God* or *the Kingdom of Heaven* have come to sound like faraway ethereal realms where God reigns over matters of privatized religion and personal moral codes. The truth is that the Kingdom of God is the government of God. The teaching of Jesus is the administration of Jesus. The fruit of the Spirit is the political platform of the Spirit. As Eugene Peterson notes, "The gospel of Jesus Christ is more political than anyone imagines, but in a way that no one guesses. The 'kingdom of God,' an altogether political metaphor, is basic vocabulary in understanding the Christian gospel."[8] The Kingdom of Heaven is a kingdom coming from heaven to earth, which is why we pray daily as Jesus taught us, "Your kingdom come. Your will be done, on earth as it is in heaven" (Matthew 6:10).

We struggle to construct a working definition of *God's Kingdom* because even though Jesus describes and announces the Kingdom through his parables, he doesn't define it. Nonetheless, we can construct a definition by gathering clues and putting them together. We can look at what the disciples believed about the Kingdom. We can also look at when, where, and how Jesus' rule would take place. Together these clues can help us more clearly define what God's Kingdom is.

Apparently Jesus' disciples knew what he meant when he talked about the Kingdom. The first-century world did not live during the secular age of separation of church and state. What we would separate into "politics" and "religion" were woven together in the very fabric of their society. Jesus' disciples believed in his ministry and his announcement of the Kingdom. In the forty-day period between Jesus' resurrection and ascension, he talked to his disciples about the Kingdom of God. We read in Acts: "So when they had come together, they asked him, 'Lord, is this the time when you will restore the kingdom to Israel?'" (Acts 1:6). They understood that Jesus wasn't bringing a heavenly kingdom for another time and place, but his Kingdom was connected to a physical, geopolitical region of the earth. They understood that the Kingdom of God was the rule of God. The disciples believed Jesus was the promised Jewish king, the Messiah or "Christ." They believed Jesus came as the embodiment of Israel's God, who desired to be the King of the world. They celebrated the rule of God over all nations in their worship: "The LORD, the Most High, is awesome, a great king over all the earth" (Psalm 47:2). If the disciples believed that God's Kingdom existed in a concrete time and place, then we should regard God's Kingdom in the same way.

The disciples' next natural question was *when* Jesus would be installed and recognized as a political king. That was the question they asked between his resurrection and ascension. They wanted to know when God was going to return to rule over Israel and the world. The question was about timing. Was now the time he was going to restore the Kingdom, that is God's rule, to the earth? The answer was yes! Jesus had come to restore God's rule to Israel for the sake of the world.

So if the reign of Jesus was to start immediately, the next question is *where*? God's Kingdom would not be limited to one strip of land east of the Mediterranean Sea. Jesus, the Son of God, would receive the nations of the world as his inheritance. We read of this inheritance in Psalm 2: "I will tell of the decree of the LORD: He said to me, 'You are my son; today I have begotten you. Ask of me, and I will make the nations your heritage, and the ends of the earth your possession'" (Psalm 2:7-8). Jesus would die and rise again as the King of Israel, but through his ascension he would be enthroned as the King of the world.

Finally, if Jesus' rule began now, and he would rule over the whole world, *what* would his reign look like? He rules all nations in a counterintuitive—and counterimperial—way. His rule is unlike that of any other ruler before or since. Jesus rules not by the love of power but in the power of love. He would rule not by slaying his enemies, but by being slain as the Lamb of God. Jesus comes announcing the Kingdom of God with plans to set up his throne. His agenda prioritizes a love for God, for neighbor, for those in need, and even for enemies. In God's Kingdom the rich and powerful serve the poor and lowly. Jesus announced the upside-down platform of God's Kingdom, where "the last will be first, and the first will be last" (Matthew 20:16). This counterintuitive nature of the Kingdom was captured in Mary's Magnificat, itself a politically charged anthem of the Kingdom:

> He has shown strength with his arm;
> > he has scattered the proud in the thoughts of their hearts.
> He has brought down the powerful from their thrones,
> > and lifted up the lowly;
> he has filled the hungry with good things,
> > and sent the rich away empty.
> LUKE 1:51-53

When we gather these clues, we can cobble together a solid definition of the Kingdom where God rules. The Kingdom of God is the present rule of God in Christ on the earth through the church.[9] The Kingdom of God isn't a synonym for heaven because the Kingdom comes from heaven to earth. The Kingdom isn't synonymous with the church. As followers of Jesus, we serve the Kingdom. We announce and demonstrate the Kingdom's power, but we are not the Kingdom.[10] The Kingdom of God is not God's limited rule over what some call personal "spiritual matters," and the Kingdom of God is not only a matter of the people's work for justice. The scope of God's Kingdom is both personal and political, touching on matters of both justification and justice.

In the end, political parties and political candidates cannot fully embody the Kingdom of God or be the way the Kingdom comes because modern American politics are fueled by coercion and wealth. To align ourselves with a political party is to defect from God's Kingdom and ally ourselves with a kingdom of this world. By contrast, Jesus announced a blessing upon the poor and the peacemakers in God's Kingdom. Modern politicos on both sides of the aisle bless wealthy donors and single-minded lobbyists.

In keeping with Mary's song, we remain in step with the radical nature of the Kingdom by centering the Lamb of God in our political engagement and by cutting ties with hope in the political parties of our day. If we choose to engage in the political process, we do so with dispassionate participation, with action without much hope in it. Our hope rests in God alone. We participate knowing that the votes we cast may help promote the common good to some degree but that real, lasting change will come from God's work through the life of the church.

NO MORE JERKS FOR JESUS

Politics has always been contentious and divisive, but modern America has abandoned nearly every attempt at civility, respect, and honor in this sector. Lampooning and demonizing political opponents has become the cultural norm. My heart breaks when I see Christians fall under the intoxicating spell of shock-jock politicians and pundits, especially when Christian leaders imitate their immature, bullying antics. There's another way to engage in the politics of this world while remaining faithful to our calling as followers of King Jesus. Our voice matters in the public square, even more so when we speak on justice and public policy. Eugene Cho is helpful in leading us forward:

> We can't merely be intellectual or cultural Christians who become pawns in a political chess game. As Christians, our integrity still matters. Our commitment to truth telling still matters. Our commitment to justice and the vulnerable still matters. Our commitment to grace and mercy still matters.
>
> Why do these things still matter?
>
> Because our commitment to Jesus *and* His ways still matters.
>
> Church, disagreeing with someone's politics, views, religion, and ideology is never permission to harass or bully that person. And certainly it's never okay to threaten their well-being. Don't do it. And don't let people you know do it.
>
> In other words, don't be a jerk for Jesus.[11]

Jesus blazed a pathway of forgiveness for us, but we must be willing to pass through the gate of confession and repentance. Take a moment to honestly review how you express your political opinions. Ask yourself if people would listen to you talk about politics and think *She's just a jerk*. Ask yourself if people who don't know you well would read your political social-media posts and say, "That guy's a jerk!" If you answer yes, then it's time to admit you have veered off the path of the Lamb.

If your passion for a certain political issue has turned you into a jerk, then it's time for a change. God forgives, but to step into that forgiveness you must repent of both your allegiance to partisanship and the harshness in which you engage in politics. Resisting the temptation to be a jerk for Jesus does not mean that we run headlong into quietism. Rather we adopt Jesus' way of civility, of honoring the dignity of other human beings, of humbly listening before we speak.

Jesus wasn't quiet when the rowdy crowd brought a woman caught in the act of adultery. But before he said, "Let anyone among you who is without sin be the first to throw a stone at her" (John 8:7), he bent down and started writing in the dirt. Before we throw our stones of political rebuttal, we pause to think before we speak. As messengers of the Lamb, we have something to say, but first we reject the spirit of our hostile age and follow the Lamb into a political posture marked by respect, civility, and concern for the common good. We certainly need the Holy Spirit's guidance in centering Jesus when we speak against social injustices and systemic sin, so that we can speak the truth in love (Ephesians 4:15). We can publicly disagree with a brother or sister in Christ without posturing ourselves as the judge of their faith. We can call out the hypocrisy or harshness we see in others' political opinions without doing so from a place of judgement. Jesus is the judge; judging is his job. We are not called to imitate Jesus in his judgment. We are called to imitate Jesus in his love.

We need less reactive social-media warriors and more carefully cultivated online civility and kindness shaped by God's Kingdom values. We need more followers of the Lamb to stand calmly as angry politicos hurl their insults. In reflection of Jesus, we respond with compassion and blessing. We cannot speak the truth of Jesus in any other way than in the way of Jesus.

Our sovereign King rules with a lamblike peace that looks very different from the political world of twenty-first-century America. God's sovereignty means that in Jesus, God is ruling the earth. God isn't controlling or determining all human action, but he is guiding human history toward his ultimate purpose—the renewal of all things. Jesus reigns now, but not everyone submits their lives to his authority. As we bear witness to Jesus' politics, we shine a light on the Kingdom of God, which has no end. Massive empires, political nations, and governments of men all come and go, but God's word and his Kingdom endure forever. The world will see the reign of the Lamb if we walk faithfully in his ways.

DISCUSSION QUESTIONS

1. What were some of the political messages you heard growing up?

2. If you have voted, when was the first time? As you reflect on that experience, do you rejoice or lament in how you voted?

3. Does the call to abandon hope in political parties challenge you? Frustrate you? Free you? Please you? Or something else?

4. How did you feel about the events at the Capitol Building on January 6, 2021? What can we do to prevent an event like this from occurring in the future?

5. Do you have any hope for a decrease in the hostility in our public discourse regarding politics? Why or why not?

6. In what ways do Jesus' teachings inform your political imagination and opinions?

7. Would people say your politics make you sound like Jesus or a jerk?

8. What can you do to be an instrument of peace in our divided and hostile world?

THE REIGN OF THE LAMB

Almighty and everlasting God, whose will it is to restore all things in your well-beloved Son, the King of kings and Lord of lords: Mercifully grant that the peoples of the earth, divided and enslaved by sin, may be freed and brought together under his most gracious rule; who lives and reigns with you and the Holy Spirit, one God, now and for ever. Amen.

A COLLECT, PROPER 29,
THE BOOK OF COMMON PRAYER

THE "HALLELUJAH" CHORUS within George Frideric Handel's epic *Messiah* has endured throughout the English-speaking world. Its melody, music, and lyrics have filtered into pop culture, appearing in commercials, TV shows, and films. The soaring chorus reaches its climax declaring the reign of King Jesus and is punctuated with echoing hallelujahs:

King of kings (Forever and ever. Hallelujah! Hallelujah!),
And Lord of lords (King of kings, and Lord of lords).

And He shall reign
And He shall reign
And He shall reign forever and ever.

King of kings! (Forever and ever.)
And He shall reign (Hallelujah! Hallelujah!)
And He shall reign forever and ever.
King of kings! And Lord of lords!
King of kings! And Lord of lords!
And He shall reign forever and ever.
Forever and ever
Forever and ever
Hallelujah! Hallelujah!
Hallelujah! Hallelujah!
Hallelujah![1]

Jennifer Marshall-Patterson describes the enduring legacy of Handel's *Messiah* as rooted in the work's lyrical content, grounding modern listeners in something both permanent and transcendent, a profound reminder that "human nature persists, truth exists and life has meaning and purpose."[2] The lyrics of *Messiah* are drawn from Scripture and emphasized by an ascending, joy-filled melody, which directs our attention to Jesus, who reigns. The majesty and celebration of the famed "Hallelujah" chorus prompts people to stand.

The words of the chorus draw on language and imagery from the book of Revelation, where we see Jesus depicted as a slain lamb (Revelation 5:6). In a surprising twist, this lamb lives! The Lamb is enthroned and worshiped (Revelation 5:11-14). The Lamb is worthy to be praised because he is ruling and reigning. After John witnesses the Lamb breaking open six of the seven seals on the scroll in his hand, a large multiethnic crowd around the throne captures John's attention:

After this I looked, and there was a great multitude that no one could count, from every nation, from all tribes and peoples and languages, standing before the throne and before the Lamb, robed in white, with palm branches in their hands. They cried out in a loud voice, saying,

"Salvation belongs to our God who is seated on the throne, and to the Lamb!"

REVELATION 7:9-10

First-century believers who felt the crushing blows of persecution for their allegiance to King Jesus heard these words in the triumphant spirit captured in Handel's *Messiah*. They knew Jesus was the Lamb of John's heavenly vision. They believed, as we do today, that he is the King of kings and Lord of lords, and that the slaughtered Lamb of God will reign forever and ever. What a *hallelujah*-worthy truth!

THE LAMB AT THE CENTER

In John's vision, he sees angels and twenty-four mysterious elders joining in this heavenly act of worship. One of the elders questions John to see if he knows who these people are who worship the Lamb with white robes on their backs and palm branches in their hands. John declines to answer, and the elder describes the crowd as those who have been washed in the blood of the Lamb. They have been stripped of their old, tattered clothes, their old identity as a people subjected to sin and death. This great crowd of people drawn from all the people of the earth have been clothed in white robes, washed clean by the Lamb's own blood. The elder speaking to John in this vision draws on the imagery of the sacrificial lamb in Jewish worship. According to the law of Moses, the blood of ritualistic sacrifice was to cleanse and purify Israel of the pollutants of idolatry, immorality, and injustice (Leviticus 16:18-19). The worshipers in John's vision have been washed clean by the blood of the Lamb, who came to take away the sin of the world and liberate people from the fear and sting of death.

In response to the freedom they have experienced from the stain of sin and the power of death, these white-robed worshipers express their heartfelt worship to the Lamb on the throne. The elder continues:

> They will hunger no more, and thirst no more;
> the sun will not strike them,
> nor any scorching heat;
> for *the Lamb at the center of the throne will be their shepherd*,
> and he will guide them to springs of the water of life,
> and God will wipe away every tear from their eyes."
> REVELATION 7:16-17, EMPHASIS ADDED

With hearts full of gratitude, people from every walk of life and every ethnicity practice an ongoing posture of worship. In their union with God, they find their deepest hunger satisfied by God's very presence. In this act of worship, they don't push the Lamb off to the periphery; the Lamb is at the center. With all the fantastic images swirling around the throne of God in John's revelation—the choir of multitudes, the elders, the angelic living creatures, the scroll, and the breaking of the seals—right in the very center is the Lamb enthroned. In their worship, they are centering Jesus.

John's heavenly vision is an earthly vision for us. All other visions and interpretations of Jesus fail to capture the essence of King Jesus, of how he rules and reigns. Jesus didn't come to rule in the way of tyrants or warriors. We may prefer a warrior king who humiliates his enemies and imposes his agenda on the world through domination and brute force, but this kind of rule is not the way the Kingdom of Jesus comes. Theologian and professor Miroslav Volf notes that what is most surprising in the book of Revelation is that "at the *center* of the throne, holding together both the throne and the whole cosmos that is ruled by the throne, we find the sacrificed *Lamb*. . . . At the very heart of 'the One who sits on the throne' is the cross."[3]

He rules as the slain Lamb, and we enter his saving rule by rejecting all other kingdoms. We turn to the Lamb who reigns with trust in our hearts and worship on our lips. We live as citizens of this Kingdom with John's vision in our hearts and with our eyes fixed on the Lamb centered on the throne.

If we place any other person, object, agenda, plan, or intention in the center, we will quickly veer off course. Idols will come, tempting us to orient our lives around something else. In Jesus' temptation in the wilderness, the devil used good things to tempt Jesus to set a course that would lead him away from the Kingdom of God. In the same way, idols often appear as good things that we can use to improve our lives, but they will always fail us in the end. Love never fails, and the Lamb who fully embodies God's love will never fail us. In fact, the Lamb who rules from his heavenly throne draws us near by his sacrificial love. Volf adds, "With the Lamb at the center of the throne, the distance between the 'throne' and the 'subjects' has collapsed in the embrace of the triune God."[4]

The Lamb at the center of the throne guides us to the springs of the water of life. This is our purpose—to experience full and abundant life. Jesus said, "Whoever believes in [God] should not perish but have eternal life," the life of the age to come (John 3:16, ESV). In guiding us toward abundant life, God will wipe away the tears from our eyes. This is our peace—to experience freedom and healing from all that seeks to damage and destroy. Jesus died carrying away our sin and sorrow in the ultimate act of sacrificial love. The way Jesus sacrifices is the way he shepherds. Jesus said:

> I am the good shepherd. The good shepherd lays down his life for the sheep. He who is a hired hand and not a shepherd, who does not own the sheep, sees the wolf

> coming and leaves the sheep and flees, and the wolf
> snatches them and scatters them. He flees because he
> is a hired hand and cares nothing for the sheep.
> JOHN 10:11-13, ESV

Jesus is no mere hired hand, someone picking up some extra hours by working on the farm. He is the Shepherd who loves his sheep, laying down his life for those he loves in order to rescue them from the wolves of sin and death, which seek to destroy them. He defeats these wolves by sacrificing himself, giving himself over to them. Jesus continued by saying, "I am the good shepherd. I know my own and my own know me, just as the Father knows me and I know the Father; and I lay down my life for the sheep" (John 10:14-15, ESV). The Lamb known as the frailest of farm animals has become the Shepherd of all who believe in him.

To experience the redemption and refreshment Jesus offers, we must continue centering Jesus. When we allow Jesus to sit front and center on the throne of our lives, our mantra becomes *King Jesus first. King Jesus foremost. King Jesus forever.* Jesus comes to rule, not with a sword in his hand but with healing in his hands, healing for the nations and healing for me and you. Jesus comes to rule not by slaying his enemies but by being slain, not by requiring blood but by offering his own, not by taking life but by giving it.

As the Lamb at the center of the throne, he takes the role of Shepherd to lead us to the good life. The life Jesus offers is not merely life without end, though it includes that. The Lamb is leading us to the life of the coming age, where we won't hurt or destroy one another anymore. Those outside the Kingdom of God perish in the misery of idolatry, but those who believe experience everlasting life. We enjoy the first taste of that life now, when we pledge our allegiance to King Jesus and find ourselves living in God's Kingdom. Within this kind of life, we experience our created purpose.

God handcrafted each one of us. "It was you who formed my inward parts," the psalmist writes, "you knit me together in my mother's womb. I praise you, for I am fearfully and wonderfully made. Wonderful are your works; that I know very well" (Psalm 139:13-14). As daughters and sons of God, we were each uniquely made in God's image to bear God's beautiful image in the world. Living as image bearers is our purpose, but sin and death have shattered that image. The Lamb of God comes to take away the sin of the world and conquer death, so that those who wash in the blood of the Lamb receive the white robe of a renewed and restored purpose. We worship God for this in the words of the old hymn:

> There is a fountain filled with blood
> Drawn from Immanuel's veins;
> And sinners, plunged beneath that flood,
> Lose all their guilty stains.[5]

With the guilt of our sin washed clean by the blood of the Lamb, we experience peace and can live according to the purpose for which we were created. With the power of sin broken and the fear of death removed, God's image on our hearts begins to be restored.

In our experience of redemption and healing, when we keep the Lamb centered in every area of our lives, we discover our purpose and experience God's peace. As we have seen, we can keep Jesus at the center of all our spiritual-formation practices. We keep Jesus central to our prayer through our practice of the Jesus Prayer. We keep Jesus at the center of our reading of all Scripture, by allowing Jesus to be our guide. None of this is done on our own. God the Holy Spirit remains at work within us, pointing us to Jesus in all we do. We also keep Jesus at the center of our moral lives as we allow the virtues of faith, hope, and love to be shaped by Jesus himself. Finally we keep Jesus at the core of our common life together as our worship life is centered on Jesus, our advocacy for justice is led by Jesus, and our political imagination is dominated and shaped by our allegiance to the Lamb.

COMING TOGETHER IN THE LIGHT OF THE LAMB

The worship of the reigning Lamb continues through John's revelation to the end. Again he sees a large crowd of heavenly worshippers, and in their act of worship, they invite us to join the Lamb in a lavish wedding reception:

> Then I heard what seemed to be the voice of a great multitude, like the sound of many waters and like the sound of mighty thunderpeals, crying out,
>
>> "Hallelujah!
>> For the Lord our God
>>   the Almighty reigns.
>> Let us rejoice and exult
>>   and give him the glory,
>> for the marriage of the Lamb has come,
>>   and his bride has made herself ready;
>> to her it has been granted to be clothed
>>   with fine linen, bright and pure"—
>> for the fine linen is the righteous deeds of the saints.
>
> And the angel said to me, "Write this: Blessed are those who are invited to the marriage supper of the Lamb." And he said to me, "These are true words of God."
> REVELATION 19:6-9

John the Revelator has slid that invitation across the table to you and to me. In our worship of the reigning Lamb of God, we are invited to step closer. We don't worship from afar; we are welcomed into a covenant, into a holy and everlasting relationship with the Lamb. Jesus is the groom, and we are the bride. In the end, our union with the Lamb will be complete. From his throne in heaven, the Lamb will come to earth to bring God's reconciling power. Heaven and earth will be reunited as the Lamb marries his bride—the church, the people of the Lamb.

John sees these final events as the re-creation of heaven and earth: "Then I saw a new heaven and a new earth; for the first heaven and the first earth had passed away, and the sea was no more" (Revelation 21:1). When heaven and earth meet in a cosmic marriage, the earth will be remade, perfected, and restored. This vision is rooted in Isaiah's prophecy:

> For as the new heavens and the new earth,
>   which I will make,
> shall remain before me, says the LORD;
>   so shall your descendants and your name remain.
> From new moon to new moon,
>   and from sabbath to sabbath,
> all flesh shall come to worship before me,
> says the LORD.
> ISAIAH 66:22-23

As with all the prophecies of the Old Testament, this one finds its fulfillment in Jesus, who brings to the marriage supper of the Lamb those whose robes have been washed in his blood.

This coming together of God and his people points to the coming together of a new heaven and a new earth, where the central activity is worship of the one true living God.[6] God will live with his people in the new heaven and new earth, a restoration of the original design for creation. God has always wanted to be present with us.

This vision is woven through the entire story of Scripture, from the Garden of Eden, where God walked the earth in the cool evening breeze (Genesis 3:8), to the new Jerusalem, where God will dwell with his people (Revelation 21:3). In one of John's final visions, he sees the new Jerusalem, a holy and heavenly city on the newly recreated earth. This city does not have a single building where people gather to worship God because the city is a temple where God dwells with his people forever.

This beautiful city of God does not need the sun to illuminate its streets, "For the glory of God is its light, and its lamp is the Lamb. The nations will walk by its light, and the kings of the earth will bring their glory into it. Its gates will never be shut by day—and there will be no night there" (Revelation 21:23-25). Imagine a city brightly illuminated not by nature's lights or man-made streetlights but by the light of God's beauty emanating from the Lamb, the true and everlasting Word of God, who is a lamp to our feet and a light to our path (Psalm 119:105). Imagine a refashioned city swept clean from the pollution of evil and the darkness of death, peacefully bathed in a brilliant light. The Lamb on the throne governs a city whose gates remain open for all who want to live in the light of God's never-ending love. This city is a picture of our future.

HOW NOW SHALL WE LIVE?

We have entered through those gates with thanksgiving in our hearts. Through our trust in and allegiance to the Lamb, we have come into this city now because we are presently sitting with Jesus in heavenly places (Ephesians 2:6). For us all things are being made new! We have been rescued by the blood of the Lamb from the old, worn-down city and are standing in the brilliant light of this new city, but what now? We recognize that while we have been rescued from this present evil age, we still have a home here. We are dual citizens in the old Jerusalem and the new Jerusalem, but the vision of the new Jerusalem where the Lamb is enthroned has forever changed us. We cannot unsee what we have seen. *So how are we to conduct our lives in this complexity? How do we live in the reign of the Lamb? Where do we go from here?* Michael Gorman describes a spirituality implicit in John's revelation that includes, among other things, worship and an "embodied communal witness and mission."[7] Our spirituality—that is, our lived experience empowered by the Holy Spirit—has been irrevocably shaped by our vision of the reign of the Lamb, so we live lives of worship, imitation, and witness.

First, *the Lamb is not inviting us to fight for him. He is inviting us to worship him.* Our life-changing encounter with the slain Lamb who rescued, the Lamb who reigns in the power of cosuffering love, evokes hearts willing to worship. Our response to the reign of the Lamb isn't raised fists but open and lifted hands. The way the Lamb saves us is the way we follow him, so for us, fighting gives way to worship. We respond with worship as a first act and as an ongoing action. We never move past worshiping the Lamb because we are living in his uncreated light every day. We maintain daily, weekly, and annual habits of worship because there is no end to the unfolding beauty of the Lamb. God made us for God's own self, as we learn from Augustine's ancient prayer,[8] and our hearts remain in a state of restlessness until, through our acts of worship, we find rest in the presence of the Father, Son, and Holy Spirit.

Second, *the Lamb is not asking us to defend him. He is asking us to imitate him.* We form a defensive posture when we fear the pain of potential loss. We know how this story is going to end—the Lamb conquers, the Lamb wins! We certainly prepare ourselves to offer a defense for the hope within us (1 Peter 3:15). A skeptical world has questions, and we can answer by expressing what we have seen and experienced, but we do so from a position of confidence in the Lamb, not fear of the world. The Lamb can't lose because God is faithful to his promise of the new creation. Instead of taking a stand *for* Jesus, we stand *with* Jesus, imitating what we see. Jesus gave his life, and so do we. Jesus served the weak and vulnerable, and so do we. Jesus brought healing wherever he went, and so do we.

Third, *the Lamb is not calling us to conquer the world for him. He is calling us to **bear witness to** him.* In an increasingly post-Christian culture in Western Europe, Canada, and the United States, the temptation we face is to use the powers of coercion, accusation, and dominance to "take back" our city, our country, or our world for Jesus. But these are methods the devil uses, not followers of Jesus. Instead we imitate Jesus, who resisted the devil in the wilderness. We find our calling in sacred Scripture: to receive the power of the Spirit and be witnesses of the Lamb (Acts 1:8). God doesn't burden us with the responsibility to conquer the world, but to bear witness to the one who has conquered, the one who has the power to change hearts and communities. From here we go and do. Marked by his lamblike image, we become people of the Lamb, living that the world might know the truth—the Lamb reigns.

In some of my most honest and vulnerable moments, when I am unsure of the cohesion of our faith or the effectiveness of the church's mission, I find myself meditating on Jesus. I envision him with outstretched arms, the sacrificial Lamb offering his life so we may truly live in a world free of injustice, oppression, brokenness, and pain. Life is hard and humanity continues to invent new ways to compound the difficulties, but I remain hopeful. Jesus Christ our King has conquered through his death and resurrection. The light of new life that burst forth from Jesus' tomb on Easter fills my heart with hope. Our job as followers of the Lamb is to endure to the end. We can and *will* endure—if we never stop centering Jesus.

DISCUSSION QUESTIONS

1. Why do you think music has the ability to capture our attention and inspire us?

2. What do the images of worship in Revelation speak to us about how we worship today?

3. When you imagine Jesus at the center of the throne, what thoughts and feelings come to mind?

4. What does Jesus as a slain lamb say about the way he shepherds and leads us?

5. How does Jesus as the Lamb serve as a light for us?

6. Why is worship of the Lamb a better response to the challenges of this world than fighting for the Lamb?

7. What would it look like for you to imitate the Lamb?

8. What is one thing you can do this week to bear witness to the Lamb?

ACKNOWLEDGMENTS

For me writing books has become a calling. I write because I am *compelled* to write. I write because I have words welling up in me. I often find myself with a head full of ideas that are driving me insane. I write specifically for the local church. I write to create conversations in churches, that the people of God would grow and mature in the ways of Jesus. I have included discussion questions with each chapter, and I pray for readers to find a small group of friends at church to read and discuss this book together.

These are hard days for the American church. The rising flood-waters of secularism, rugged individualism, and the rise of white Christian nationalism pose a real threat. Attendance in church gatherings continues to trend downward, especially after the pandemic. But I believe Jesus, the Lamb of God, is with us. Jesus promised to be with us to the end of the age (Matthew 28:20). And I believe in the local church. I offer this book as a way for the church in America to rediscover its identity as people who follow the Lamb and walk in his ways.

While writing is in one sense a solo project, it is hardly done in isolation. Books like this one have grown out of countless sermons, online articles, teachings, and conversations I have had with people at my church. I am thankful for Word of Life Church, both the in-person congregation that gathers in St. Joseph, Missouri, and our online congregation made up of sincere Jesus followers from all over the US, Canada, and Europe. I'm particularly thankful for those who participated in my online small group on "The Lamb at the Center" in early 2021. Our conversations surrounding this captivating image of Jesus as the Lamb of God shaped the contents of this book. Many of those beloved participants like Pam Henderson, Chris Orozco, and Pete Swanberg have encouraged me and still encourage me today.

I'm fortunate to have found like-minded pastors and thinkers who have shaped me as a pastor and writer. Brad Jersak, Brian Zahnd, Derwin Gray, and Rich Villodas are some of the thinkers and authors who have given shape to this present book. I'm forever grateful for the work of Tom Wright, my theological mentor from afar. It seems everything I write has his fingerprints all over it. Two men I highly admire passed away while I was writing this book—Orthodox Metropolitan Kallistos Ware and Pentecostal theologian Gordon Fee. I quote both men in this book, and they represent two very different theological and ecclesiological traditions which have influenced me greatly. They live on in blessed memory and in the pages of this book.

Centering Jesus would have never come into being if it wasn't for the great team at NavPress. I was seventeen years old when I went through my first NavPress workbook in a small group of teenagers. Now, some thirty years leader, NavPress is publishing this book. I am honored.

The NavPress team gave me the term *centering Jesus*, which became the title and a key term I integrated through the book. I'm thankful for David Zimmerman, who believed in this project and gave me helpful suggestions on the book's structure. It was David's idea to take much of the material I had written on the Lamb in Revelation and make it the concluding chapter. That suggestion made for a great ending to the book! I appreciate Adam Graber's thoughtful editorial insight. He helped me sharpen my focus, with great attention to the book's cohesion. Adam helped me refine this project from a reader's perspective. I am also indebted to Elizabeth Schroll's careful attention to details throughout this book. Elizabeth's corrections and helpful suggestions made this a better book. I'm also grateful for her many words of encouragement during the editorial process. Much thanks to my editor, Deborah Sáenz Gonzalez, for her encouragement and guidance throughout the writing of this book. Working with her on this book was a delight.

Finally I want to give one grand shout-out to my family. Having a husband and dad who writes on top of serving as a pastor requires some sacrifice on their part. Jenni, Taylor, and Dylan: Thank you for giving me the time and space to write. Thank you for understanding when I had to forsake time together to write and edit. Thanks also to my son Wesley and daughter-in-law Maggie, who gave me my first grandchild. Leo Edward Vreeland was born during the editing phase of this book. (In fact, on the day he was born, I spent nearly the entire day editing.)

The birth of my first grandchild has deepened my sense of urgency and necessity for this book. I want to see the work of King Jesus flourish not only in my generation now but also in Leo's generation in the future. I see it as a colossal failure if we only cultivate the faith in our generation and do not pass it on to generations to come. I do not want it said of us that "another generation grew up after them, who did not know the LORD" (Judges 2:10). To that end, I write for my grandson and his generation, that they may come to follow the Lamb with all their lives.

Leo, D-Pa loves you. This book is dedicated to you.

NOTES

PRELUDE

1. Johnny Cash, "What Is Truth," *What Is Truth / Sing a Traveling Song* © 1970 Columbia.
2. Dorothy A. Connor, "Our Lamb Has Conquered," *Moravian Book of Worship*, 1995.

CHAPTER 1 | THE CURIOUS CASE OF THE DIMINISHING LAMB

1. Photo taken by J. Patout Burns Jr. Included here with his permission. "St. Vitale—Agnus Dei" is part of Art in the Christian Tradition, a project of the Vanderbilt Divinity Library, https://diglib.library.vanderbilt.edu/act -imagelink.pl?RC=31930.
2. A stained-glass window at the Rights Chapel of Trinity Moravian Church in Winston-Salem, North Carolina. Photo taken by JJackman. Image shared under Creative Commons license CC-BY-SA 3.0 (https://creativecommons .org/licenses/by-sa/3.0/legalcode).
3. *The Book of Common Prayer and Administration of the Sacraments with Other Rites and Ceremonies of the Church According to the Use of the Anglican Church in North America, Together with the New Coverdale Psalter* (Huntington Beach, CA: Anglican Liturgy Press, 2019), 96.
4. Kari Jobe, "Revelation Song," *Kari Jobe* © 2009 Integrity Music. From Revelation 5:12, ESV.
5. Kristin Kobes Du Mez, *Jesus and John Wayne: How White Evangelicals Corrupted a Faith and Fractured a Nation* (New York: Liveright, 2020), 10–11.
6. David E. Fitch, *The Church of Us vs. Them: Freedom from a Faith That Feeds on Making Enemies* (Grand Rapids, MI: Brazos Press, 2019), 187.
7. *Unalienable rights* and *pursuit of Happiness*: from the Declaration of Independence; *liberty and justice for all*: from the Pledge of Allegiance.

8. For more see David E. Fitch, *The End of Evangelicalism?: Discerning a New Faithfulness for Mission* (Eugene, OR: Cascade Books, 2011), 22–39.

9. Adapted from the Apostles' Creed, which has its origins in the early centuries of the church.

10. Fitch, *Church of Us vs. Them*, 116.

11. Fitch, *Church of Us vs. Them*, 30–34.

CHAPTER 2 | BEHOLD THE LAMB

1. According to Scot McKnight, "To call Jesus Son of God, then, was to say he was the Messianic King. This . . . use is just what a normal Jewish reader of the Bible would think. 'Son of God' in the Old Testament is a title used for the king of Israel. It begins when God calls David his son (2 Sam. 7:8-16), but my favorite expression is found in Psalm 2:7: 'You are my son; today I have become your father.' On top of this, the whole Roman Empire referred to Caesar Augustus as the son of God." Scot McKnight, *Kingdom Conspiracy: Returning to the Radical Mission of the Local Church* (Grand Rapids, MI: Brazos, 2014), 132. See also N. T. Wright, *Jesus and the Victory of God* (Minneapolis: Fortress Press, 1996), 485; and Matthew W. Bates, *Gospel Allegiance: What Faith in Jesus Misses for Salvation in Christ* (Grand Rapids, MI: Brazos, 2019), 42.

2. See Hebrews 11:28, which speaks of this mysterious "Destroyer."

3. Michael J. Gorman, *Reading Revelation Responsibly: Uncivil Worship and Witness: Following the Lamb into the New Creation* (Eugene, OR: Cascade Books, 2011), 109.

4. Dana M. Harris, "Portraits of King Jesus in the Book of Revelation," in *Living the King Jesus Gospel: Discipleship and Ministry Then and Now*, ed. Nijay K. Gupta et al. (Eugene, OR: Cascade Books, 2021), 106.

5. John Mark Comer, *The Ruthless Elimination of Hurry* (Colorado Springs: Waterbrook, 2019), 222.

INTERLUDE | SPIRITUAL FORMATION

1. Dallas Willard, *Renovation of the Heart: Putting on the Character of Christ* (Colorado Springs: NavPress, 2002), 22.

2. I give a fuller description of "spiritual pathways" as a metaphor for spiritual disciplines in *By the Way: Getting Serious about Following Jesus* (Harrisonburg, VA: Herald Press, 2019), 150–153.

CHAPTER 3 | THE JESUS PRAYER

1. I describe my discovery of liturgical prayer in *By the Way: Getting Serious about Following Jesus* (Harrisonburg, VA: Herald Press, 2019), 186–187.

2. The instruction to pray the Lord's Prayer three times a day is found in the *Didache*, an early Christian document from the first century. See https://www .newadvent.org/fathers/0714.htm.

3. I appreciate that the Southern Baptists not only teach us to pray with the Scripture, but they also teach Christians to pray for peace and "do all in their power to put an end to war." Article XVI, entitled "Peace and War" in the *Baptist Faith and Message 2000* calls on followers of Jesus to pray peace prayers: "Christian people throughout the world should pray for the reign of the Prince of Peace." See https://bfm.sbc.net/bfm2000/#xvi.

4. For additional prayers for mercy, see also Matthew 9:27; 15:21-22; 17:14-16; 20:29-31; and Luke 17:11-13; 18:37-39. The prayer for mercy is also found in Psalm 51:1 and 123:3.

5. In the Orthodox tradition, Kallistos (Timothy) Ware bore the title "metropolitan," which is similar to "archbishop" in Western churches.

6. Kallistos Ware, *The Jesus Prayer* (London: Catholic Truth Society, 2017), 5.

7. Frederica Mathewes-Green, *The Jesus Prayer: The Ancient Desert Prayer That Tunes the Heart to God* (Brewster, MA: Paraclete Press, 2009), 9.

8. The Greek word *battalogeō* is used in the New Testament only this one time in Matthew's Gospel. It is translated "heap up empty phrases" in the NRSV and the ESV and "babble on" in the NLT.

9. Mathews-Green, *Jesus Prayer*, 33.

10. Ware, *Jesus Prayer*, 21.

11. *Hesychastic*: From the Greek word *hēsychia*, translated "quietness." Hesychastic prayer is a form of Christian prayer that emphasizes posture and controlled breathing. The goal is stillness and contemplation. According to John Michael Talbot, "A pond is a good analogy for hesychia. When the waters are still, we can look clearly into the depths of the pond, and the surface beautifully reflects an image almost flawlessly. When the waters are agitated both are jeopardized. Sacred stillness allows us to see clearly into the pond of our soul, and allows the pond to reflect the beautiful image of God in Christ." *The Jesus Prayer: A Cry for Mercy, A Path of Renewal* (Downers Grove, IL: InterVarsity Press, 2013), 146.

CHAPTER 4 | A JESUS-CENTERED READING OF SCRIPTURE

1. Michael F. Bird, *Seven Things I Wish Christians Knew about the Bible* (Grand Rapids, MI: Zondervan, 2021), 96–97.

2. Bird, *Seven Things*, 190.

3. As quoted (and translated) in Kevin J. Vanhoozer, *The Drama of Doctrine: A Canonical-Linguistic Approach to Christian Theology* (Louisville, KY: Westminster John Knox Press, 2005), 116.

4. Taken from the Nicene Creed as quoted in *The Book of Common Prayer*, 326–327.

5. *The Book of Common Prayer*, 327.

6. Irenaeus, *Against Heresies*, IV.26.1, trans. Alexander Roberts and William Rambaut, https://www.newadvent.org/fathers/0103426.htm.

7. From Augustine's Second Homily on 1 John, as quoted by David Lyle Jeffrey, *Luke* (Grand Rapids, MI: Brazos Press, 2012), 287.

8. See John 5:46.

9. Bradley Jersak, *A More Christlike Word: Reading Scripture the Emmaus Way* (New Kensington, PA: Whitaker House, 2021), 141.

10. Jersak, *A More Christlike Word*, 141.

11. Thomas Aquinas, *Summa Theologica* 1.1.10, as quoted in Jersak, *A More Christlike Word*, 131. Aquinas divides the meaning of Scripture into two senses: the literal and the spiritual, but he then subdivides the literal into three senses. In total Aquinas's division and subdivision created four different senses—or meanings—of Scripture. Aquinas describes these senses as drawing their orientation from Jesus: "So far as the things of the Old Law signify the things of the New Law, there is the *allegorical sense*; so far as the things done in Christ, or so far as the things which signify Christ, are types of what we ought to do, there is the *moral sense*. But so far as they signify what relates to eternal glory, there is the *anagogical sense*" (emphasis added); trans. Fathers of the English Dominican Province, https://www.newadvent.org/summa/1001 .htm#article10.

12. The word *anagogical* comes from the Greek word *anagoge*, meaning to climb or ascend. This sense of Scripture belongs to a devotional or "spiritual" reading, whereby the Holy Spirit uses Holy Scripture to draw our hearts toward God, to ascend toward union with God. I prefer to describe this kind of reading as "mystical" or "contemplative."

13. Consistency in daily Bible reading has come to me from my discovery of the Daily Office Lectionary, a two-year cycle through most of the Bible. This lectionary is not to be confused with the Revised Common Lectionary, which is a three-year cycle with Scripture readings for Sunday-morning worship. There are a number of slightly different versions of the Daily Office Lectionary. I follow the one provided in *The Book of Common Prayer*, 934–995, and have incorporated it into my morning prayer time with much delight. The Daily Office Lectionary provides Psalms, Old Testament, Epistle, and Gospel readings (in that order) for each day. Perhaps what I appreciate most about the lectionary tradition of Bible reading is the order, because every morning the last thing I read from Scripture are the words of Jesus. My peace is renewed every morning as Jesus receives my full attention.

CHAPTER 5 | THE SPIRIT POINTS US TO JESUS

1. Michael Lipka and Claire Gecewicz, "More Americans Now Say They're Spiritual but Not Religious," Pew Research Center, September 6, 2017, https://www.pewresearch.org/fact-tank/2017/09/06/more-americans-now-say -theyre-spiritual-but-not-religious/.

2. According to a 2021 Gallup Poll report, "Americans' membership in houses of worship continued to decline last year, dropping below 50% for the first time

in Gallup's eight-decade trend. In 2020, 47% of Americans said they belonged to a church, synagogue or mosque, down from 50% in 2018 and 70% in 1999." Jeffrey M. Jones, "U.S. Church Membership Falls Below Majority for First Time," Gallup, March 20, 2021, https://news.gallup.com/poll/341963 /church-membership-falls-below-majority-first-time.aspx.

3. Scot McKnight and Laura Barringer, *A Church Called Tov: Forming a Goodness Culture That Resists Abuses of Power and Promotes Healing* (Carol Stream, IL: Tyndale Momentum, 2020), 30–31.

4. See N. T. Wright, *Broken Signposts: How Christianity Makes Sense of the World* (New York: HarperOne, 2020), 61–65.

5. James K. A. Smith, *You Are What You Love: The Spiritual Power of Habit* (Grand Rapids, MI: Brazos Press, 2016), 23.

6. Gordon D. Fee, *God's Empowering Presence: The Holy Spirit in the Letters of Paul* (Peabody, MA: Hendrickson, 1994), 29.

7. Fee, *God's Empowering Presence*, 32.

8. Raniero Cantalamessa, *Come, Creator Spirit: Meditations on the* Veni Creator, trans. Denis and Marlene Barrett (Collegeville, MN: Liturgical Press, 2003), 57.

9. See Francis Chan with Danae Yankoski, *Forgotten God: Reversing Our Tragic Neglect of the Holy Spirit* (Colorado Springs: David C. Cook, 2009).

10. This popular concept of the Trinity is rooted in Augustine's explanation of the relational nature of love and the requirement of "three things." Augustine reflected, "Well then, when I, who make this inquiry, love anything, there are three things concerned—myself, and that which I love, and love itself. For I do not love love, except I love a lover; for there is no love where nothing is loved. Therefore there are three things—he who loves, and that which is loved, and love"; *On the Trinity*, IX.2.2, trans. Arthur West Haddan, https://www. newadvent.org/fathers/130109.htm.

11. Augustine remarked, "And the Holy Spirit, according to the Holy Scriptures, is neither of the Father alone, nor of the Son alone, but of both; and so intimates to us a mutual love, wherewith the Father and the Son reciprocally love one another"; *On the Trinity*, XV.17.27, trans. Arthur West Haddan, https://www .newadvent.org/fathers/130115.htm.

12. The Nicene Creed (AD 381).

13. Irenaeus wrote, "Now God shall be glorified in His handiwork, fitting it so as to be conformable to, and modeled after, His own Son. For by the hands of the Father, that is, by the Son and the Holy Spirit, man, and not [merely] a part of man, was made in the likeness of God"; *Against Heresies*, V.6.1, trans. Alexander Roberts and William Rambaut, https://www.newadvent.org/fathers /0103506.htm.

14. Colin E. Gunton, *Theology through the Theologians* (London: T&T Clark, 2003), 128.

15. As quoted in Cantalamessa, *Come, Creator Spirit*, 5.

16. NLT: "settling on him;" CEB: "resting on him"; ESV: "coming to rest on him"; CEV: "coming down on him."
17. "Turn Your Eyes upon Jesus," Helen Howarth Lemmel, 1922. Public domain.
18. Eugene H. Peterson, *Subversive Spirituality* (Grand Rapids, MI: Eerdmans, 1997), 37.

INTERLUDE | CHRISTIAN VIRTUES
1. Rowan Williams, *Being Disciples: Essentials of the Christian Life* (Grand Rapids, MI: Eerdmans, 2016), 35.

CHAPTER 6 | THE FOUR SIDES OF FAITH
1. Joseph J. Kotva Jr., *The Christian Case for Virtue Ethics* (Washington, DC: Georgetown University Press, 1996), 26.
2. Philosophy professor Alasdair MacIntyre defines *virtue* as "an acquired human quality the possession and exercise of which tends to enable us to achieve those goods which are internal to practices"; *After Virtue: A Study in Moral Theory*, 3rd ed. (Notre Dame, IN: University of Notre Dame Press, 2007), 191. The good which virtue enables us to obtain is the good life, that is, the virtuous life. These moral goods are contained within the practices we live out in our day-to-day lives. Kotva argues that virtue ethics do indeed maintain a focus on right or moral behavior, but that character and behavior have a symbiotic relationship. He adds, "'Being' precedes 'doing,' but 'doing' shapes 'being'"; *Christian Case for Virtue Ethics*, 30.
3. I want to avoid what James K. A. Smith calls "thinking-thingism," the belief that education alone is what we need to become good and virtuous people. I agree with Smith that our moral decision making is driven by our loves, that is, our hearts. Nevertheless our core beliefs, in addition to our habits, shape our hearts. Beliefs, among other elements, determine the kind of people we are becoming. See James K. A. Smith, *You Are What You Love: The Spiritual Power of Habit* (Grand Rapids, MI: Brazos, 2016), 5–7.
4. See Matthew 28:16-17 for an example of this.
5. Tim Keller observes that "skeptics must learn to look for a type of faith hidden within their reasoning. All doubts, however skeptical and cynical they may seem, are really a set of alternate beliefs. You cannot doubt Belief A except from a position of faith in Belief B."; *The Reason for God: Belief in an Age of Skepticism* (New York: Penguin Books, 2018), xxiv.
6. According to the Thayer's Greek-English Lexicon of the New Testament, *hupostasis* is a common Greek word that in its New Testament usage refers to "that which has foundation, is firm, hence, that which has actual existence; a substance, real being." It therefore carries the metaphorical imagery of a foundation or substructure. See Joseph Henry Thayer, *A Greek-English Lexicon of the New Testament* (New York: Harper & Brothers, 1889), 645.

7. Gregory A. Boyd, *Benefit of the Doubt: Breaking the Idol of Certainty* (Grand Rapids, MI: Baker Books, 2013), 126.

8. "Just as the body without the spirit is dead, so faith without works is also dead" (James 2:26).

9. Matthew W. Bates, *Salvation by Allegiance Alone: Rethinking Faith, Works, and the Gospel of Jesus the King* (Grand Rapids, MI: Baker Academic, 2017), 77. The Greek word *pistis*, most often translated "faith," does not always mean allegiance, but it does, according to Bates, when referring to "how the gospel of Jesus unleashes God's power for salvation"; *Salvation by Allegiance Alone*, 78.

10. Bates, *Salvation by Allegiance Alone*, 86.

CHAPTER 7 | HOPE IN THE AGE TO COME

1. *The Shawshank Redemption*, directed by Frank Darabont (Beverly Hills: Castle Rock Entertainment, 1994). Darabont's screenplay is an adaptation of a novella by Stephen King. The letter from Andy, including the description of hope as "maybe the best of things," is a near word-for-word reproduction of the letter in the novella. See Stephen King, *Rita Hayworth and Shawshank Redemption* (New York: Scribner, 2020), 109–110.

2. This definition is drawn from Glenn's comprehensive definition of Christian hope as "a confident assurance (act), grounded in God's promise and faithfulness as revealed in the Scriptures in general and in Christ in particular (grounds), that the triune God (agency) will bring about the 'resurrection of the dead and the life of the world to come' (object) at Christ's appearing (time), making heaven and earth new and one (space), by means of what has already been accomplished at the resurrection of Jesus (pathway)." Glenn Packiam, *Worship and the World to Come: Exploring Christian Hope in Contemporary Worship* (Downers Grove, IL: IVP Academic, 2020), 85.

3. N. T. Wright, *Surprised by Hope: Rethinking Heaven, the Resurrection, and the Mission of the Church* (New York: HarperOne, 2008), 41. Wright notes that his oft repeated statement about heaven not being the "end of the world" is drawn from David Lawrence, *Heaven: It's Not the End of the World! The Biblical Promise of a New Earth* (London: Scripture Union, 1995).

4. Blue Letter Bible, "Lexicon: Strong's G2015—*epiphaneia*," accessed September 16, 2022, https://www.blueletterbible.org/lexicon/g2015/esv/tr/0-1/.

5. Nicene Creed as quoted in *The Book of Common Prayer*, 326–327.

6. New Testament examples of the language of "this age" and the "age to come" include: Matthew 13:49; 24:3; 28:20; Mark 10:30; 1 Corinthians 2:8; Galatians 1:4; Ephesians 1:20-21; and Hebrews 6:5; 9:26.

7. Isaiah's vision of peace in 65:25 is also found in Isaiah 11:9: "They will not hurt or destroy on all my holy mountain; for the earth will be full of the knowledge of the LORD as the waters cover the sea." It's also found earlier in Isaiah 2:4 and 9:5-7.

CHAPTER 8 | LOVE IN THE WAY OF THE LAMB

1. Specifically, Aquinas wrote, "These theological virtues surpass the nature of man. . . . by participation, as kindled wood partakes of the nature of fire: and thus, after a fashion, man becomes a partaker of the Divine Nature, as stated above: so that these virtues are proportionate to man in respect of the Nature of which he is made a partaker"; ST I-II, Q 62, A 1, ad. 1., trans. Fathers of the English Dominican Province, https://www.newadvent.org/summa/2062.htm.

2. In the following section, I am quoting Paul in 1 Corinthians 13:3-10, MSG.

3. According to Willard, "[Love] is *not* an action, nor a feeling or emotion, nor, indeed, an intention, as 'intention' is ordinarily understood—though it gives rise to intentions and to actions of a certain type, and is associated with some 'feelings' and resistant to others. It is this understanding of *agape* love as *an overall disposition of the human self* that, alone, does justice to the teachings of Jesus and Paul and the New Testament about love and gives us *a coherent idea of love that can be aimed at in practice and implemented.* Such love is holistic, not something one turns on or off for this or that person or thing. Its orientation is toward life as a whole." Dallas Willard, *Getting Love Right* (self-published, 2012, from a paper presented at the American Association of Christian Counselors conference, Nashville, TN, September 15, 2007), n.p.

4. N. T. Wright, *After You Believe: Why Christian Character Matters* (New York: HarperOne, 2012), 182.

5. Wright, *After You Believe*, 183.

6. John Wesley described the call of Methodist preachers as: "to spread scriptural holiness over the land." As quoted by Henry H. Knight III, "Consider Wesley: 'To Spread Scriptural Holiness over the Land,'" *Catalyst* (online newsletter), April 1, 2007, https://www.catalystresources.org/consider-wesley-37/.

7. John Wesley, *A Plain Account of Christian Perfection* (Kansas City, MO: Beacon Hill Press, 1966), 51.

8. John Wesley, *Wesley's Notes on the Bible*, public domain, accessed September 21, 2022, https://www.ccel.org/ccel/wesley/notes.i.ii.v.html.

9. For Cyprian's take on habits see Alan Kreider, *The Patient Ferment of the Early Church: The Improbable Rise of Christianity in the Roman Empire* (Grand Rapids, MI: Baker Academic, 2016), 136–139, 161–170.

10. Stanley Hauerwas, "Why Community Is Dangerous: An Interview," *Plough Quarterly*, May 19, 2016, https://www.plough.com/en/topics/community/church-community/why-community-is-dangerous.

11. See Gary Chapman, *The 5 Love Languages: The Secret to Love that Lasts* (Chicago: Northfield Publishing, 2015).

12. I have adapted this concept from David Augsburger, who wrote, "Being heard is so close to being loved that for the average person, they are almost indistinguishable." As quoted in Peter Scazzero with Warren Bird, *The

Emotionally Healthy Church: A Strategy for Discipleship That Actually Changes Lives (Grand Rapids, MI: Zondervan, 2010), 190.

13. See Desmond Tutu, *No Future Without Forgiveness* (New York: Doubleday, 2000), 165.

14. Martin Luther King Jr., "Letter from Birmingham City Jail," in *A Testament of Hope: The Essential Writings and Speeches of Martin Luther King, Jr.*, ed. James Melvin Washington (New York: HarperSanFrancisco, 1991), 290.

INTERLUDE | OUR COMMON LIFE TOGETHER

1. Martin Luther King Jr., "Letter from Birmingham City Jail," in *A Testament of Hope: The Essential Writings and Speeches of Martin Luther King, Jr.*, ed. James Melvin Washington (New York: HarperSanFrancisco, 1991), 290.

CHAPTER 9 | A JESUS KIND OF CHURCH

1. Calvin described two marks of the church which shaped the entire Protestant church in all its many iterations. He argued, "Wherever we see the word of God sincerely preached and heard, wherever we see the sacraments administered according to the institution of Christ, there we cannot have any doubt that the Church of God has some existence, since his promise cannot fail, 'Where two or three are gathered together in my name, there am I in the midst of them' (Mt. 18:20)"; *Institutes of the Christian Religion*, 4.1.9, ed. John T. McNeill, trans. Ford Lewis Battles (Philadelphia: Westminster Press, 1960), 1023.

2. Tara Beth Leach, *Radiant Church: Restoring the Credibility of Our Witness* (Downers Grove, IL: IVP, 2021), 39–40.

3. Bobby Gross, *Living the Christian Year: Time to Inhabit the Story of God* (Downers Grove, IL: IVP Books, 2009), 321–322.

4. A bulleted list explaining the church year is also offered in Corey Widmer, "Telling Time Differently as Christ Followers," *Third Church* (blog), accessed November 10, 2022, https://www.thirdrva.org/blog/telling-time-differently-as-christ-followers.

5. The popular carol "The Twelve Days of Christmas" is based in this tradition of a twelve-day celebration.

6. Gross, *Living the Christian Year*, 64.

7. Second Thessalonians 1:8 particularly notes pending judgment for those who "do not obey the gospel of our Lord Jesus."

8. See Vreeland, *By the Way: Getting Serious about Following Jesus* (Harrisonburg, VA: Herald Press, 2019), 29–30.

9. John Wesley, "Sermon 101: The Duty of Constant Communion," Christian Classics Ethereal Library, accessed September 22, 2022, https://www.ccel.org/ccel/wesley/sermons.vi.xlviii.html.

10. Tara Beth Leach, *Radiant Church*, 64.

CHAPTER 10 | JUSTICE IN THE PEACEABLE KINGDOM OF GOD

1. Chris Marshall, *The Little Book of Biblical Justice* (New York: Good Books, 2005), 5–6.

2. Jessica Nicholas, *God Loves Justice: A User-Friendly Guide to Biblical Justice and Righteousness* (Los Angeles: S&E Educational Press, 2017), 21.

3. William Sanford LaSor, David Allan Hubbard, and Frederic William Bush, *Old Testament Survey: The Message, Form, and Background of the Old Testament* (Grand Rapids, MI: Eerdmans, 1982), 391.

4. According to Timothy Keller, "In the Bible *tzadeqah* refers to day-to-day living in which a person conducts *all* relationships in family and society with fairness, generosity, and equity"; *Generous Justice: How God's Grace Makes Us Just* (New York: Riverhead, 2012), 10.

5. Jessica Nicholas, *God Loves Justice*, 112.

6. Rich Villodas, *The Deeply Formed Life: Five Transformative Values to Root Us in the Way of Jesus* (Colorado Springs: WaterBrook, 2021), 201.

7. Derwin L. Gray, *God, Do You Hear Me?: Discover the Prayer God Always Answers* (Nashville: B&H Publishing, 2021), 72.

8. I am following N. T. Wright's translation, "the life of the age to come," for the common Greek phrase *zoen aionion*. Wright observes that the phrase *eternal life* can be misleading. In his commentary on Romans 5:21, Wright explains, "the normal translation, 'eternal life,' where I have put 'the life of the age to come,' gives most modern readers the quite wrong impression that Paul is talking about spending 'eternity' in a world beyond space, time and matter, in 'heaven.' Paul never mentions such an idea. What he has in mind, here and elsewhere, is the bodily resurrection of God's people to share in the new earth and new heavens"; *Paul for Everyone: Romans, Part 1* (Louisville: Westminster John Knox Press, 2004), 96.

9. Paul continues in his letter to describe the "wrath of God" that falls on the disobedient (Ephesians 5:6). God's anger is not a literal attribute of God, but a metaphor for his act of judgment. *Wrath of God* is anthropomorphic. In Romans 3 Paul uses the phrase "inflict wrath on us," which is followed in most English transitions with a parenthetical statement "I speak in a human way" (Romans 3:5). Humanly speaking, God "inflicts wrath on us," but literally what God does is judge us—and all God's acts of judgment flow out of who God is, which is love. For a fuller explanation see Bradley Jersak, *A More Christlike God: A More Beautiful Gospel* (Pasadena: Plain Truth Ministries, 2015), 183–264.

10. John Perkins and Shane Blackshear, *Go and Do: Nine Axioms on Peacemaking and Transformation from the Life of John Perkins* (Eugene, OR: Cascade Books, 2022), 13.

11. Perkins and Blackshear, *Go and Do*, 14.

12. John M. Perkins, *Let Justice Roll Down* (Ventura, CA: Regal, 1976), 194–196.

13. Rich Villodas, *The Deeply Formed Life*, 50.

CHAPTER 11 | NOT A DONKEY OR AN ELEPHANT BUT A LAMB

1. In a 2020 interview, evangelist Franklin Graham said, "I don't think evangelicals are united on every position the president takes or says, but they do recognize he is the most pro-life-friendly president in modern history." Elana Schor and Emily Swanson, "Poll: White Evangelicals Distinct on Abortion, LGBT Policy," AP News, January 2, 2020, https://apnews.com /article/donald-trump-us-news-ap-top-news-elections-immigration -8d3eb99934accc2ad795aca0183290a7.

2. "President Trump Video Statement on Capitol Protestors," C-SPAN, January 6, 2021, https://www.c-span.org/video/?507774-1/president-trump-claims -election-stolen-tells-protesters-leave-capitol.

3. Makini Brice and David Morgan, "After Not-Guilty Vote, McConnell Says Trump 'Morally Responsible' for Capitol Riot," Reuters, February 13, 2021, https://www.reuters.com/article/us-usa-trump-impeachment-republicans/after -not-guilty-vote-mcconnell-says-trump-morally-responsible-for-capitol-riot -idUSKBN2AD0OG.

4. Lee C. Camp, *Scandalous Witness: A Little Political Manifesto for Christians* (Grand Rapids, MI: Eerdmans, 2020), 100.

5. Cramer and Werntz write, "First, Christian nonviolence (as imitation of Jesus) becomes a practice by which we are formed into the image of Christ. Not only are nonviolent Christians trained to be virtuous people—courageous in the face of danger, for example—but through habits of nonviolence, their natural passions and desires are refocused toward Christ. Second, if action is what displays the full range of the virtues, then Christian nonviolence shows the world what it means to be fully human. . . . Becoming a virtuous person is inextricable from the practice of nonviolence"; *A Field Guide to Christian Nonviolence: Key Thinkers, Activists, and Movements for the Gospel of Peace* (Grand Rapids, MI: Baker Academic, 2022), 32.

6. N. T. Wright, *The Day the Revolution Began: Reconsidering the Meaning of Jesus's Crucifixion* (New York: HarperOne, 2018), 365.

7. Eugene Cho, *Thou Shalt Not Be a Jerk: A Christian's Guide to Engaging Politics* (Colorado Springs: David C Cook, 2020), 23.

8. Eugene H. Peterson, *Reversed Thunder: The Revelation of John and the Praying Imagination* (New York: HarperSanFrancisco, 1991), 117.

9. I appreciate Scot McKnight's inclusion of the church in a biblical definition of the Kingdom of God because Kingdom language includes not only the rule of the King but also the realm over which the King rules. See McKnight, *Kingdom Conspiracy* (Grand Rapids, MI: Brazos, 2014), 11–13.

10. While the body of Christ serves as servants and messengers of the Kingdom, we do not "build the Kingdom." Sometimes the phrase "build the Kingdom" is used in ecumenical circles to describe the network of churches across denominational lines. I am deeply sympathetic to this ecumenical spirit, but the catholicity of the church, that is, the unity of one holy, catholic, and

apostolic church isn't what biblical writers mean by "the Kingdom of God." We do, in the words of N. T. Wright, build *for* the Kingdom, but we recognize that God is the one to build his Kingdom. See N. T. Wright, *Surprised by Hope: Rethinking Heaven, the Resurrection, and the Mission of the Church* (New York: HarperOne, 2008), 207–208.

11. Eugene Cho, *Thou Shalt Not*, 58.

CHAPTER 12 | THE REIGN OF THE LAMB

1. George Frideric Handel, "Hallelujah," from *Messiah*, 1741, public domain.
2. Jennifer A. Marshall, "Why Handel's 'Messiah' Endures," Heritage Foundation, December 16, 2011, https://www.heritage.org/civil-society/commentary/why-handels-messiah-endures.
3. Miroslav Volf, *Exclusion and Embrace: A Theological Exploration of Identity, Otherness, and Reconciliation* (Nashville: Abingdon Press, 1996), 300. As quoted in Fleming Rutledge, *The Crucifixion: Understanding the Death of Jesus Christ* (Grand Rapids, MI: Eerdmans, 2015), 382–383.
4. Volf, *Exclusion and Embrace*, 301. I appreciate Fleming Rutledge making me aware of Volf's discussion of the Lamb at the center in her discussion of the Christus Victor theme of atonement in her book *The Crucifixion*, 383.
5. William Cowper, "Praise for the Fountain Opened," 1772, public domain.
6. This same vision of the creation of a new heavens and new earth was described by Peter. See 2 Peter 3:13.
7. Michael J. Gorman, *Reading Revelation Responsibly: Uncivil Worship and Witness: Following the Lamb into the New Creation* (Eugene, OR: Cascade Books, 2011), 178.
8. "You stir man to take pleasure in praising you, because you have made us for yourself, and our heart is restless until it rests in you"; Augustine, *Confessions*, trans. Henry Chadwick (Oxford: Oxford University Press, 2008), 3.

NavPress is the book-publishing arm of The Navigators.

Since 1933, The Navigators has helped people around the world bring hope and purpose to others in college campuses, local churches, workplaces, neighborhoods, and hard-to-reach places all over the world, face-to-face and person-by-person in an approach we call Life-to-Life® discipleship. We have committed together to know Christ, make Him known, and help others do the same.®

Would you like to join this adventure of discipleship and disciplemaking?

- Take a Digital Discipleship Journey at **navigators.org/disciplemaking**.
- Get more discipleship and disciplemaking content at **thedisciplemaker.org**.
- Find your next book, Bible, or discipleship resource at **navpress.com**.

 @NavPressPublishing

 @NavPress

 @navpressbooks